Fault Lines
of Nationhood

cross-border talks

Fault Lines
of Nationhood

gyanendra pandey
yunas samad

series editor
david page

LOTUS COLLECTION
ROLI BOOKS

~

In memory of Hamza Alavi,
distinguished scholar, friend and concerned citizen

~

Lotus Collection

© Gyanendra Pandey & Yunas Samad, 2007

First published in 2007
The Lotus Collection
An imprint of Roli Books Pvt. Ltd.
M-75, G.K. II Market, New Delhi 110 048
Phones: ++91 (011) 2921 2271, 2921 2782
2921 0886, Fax: ++91 (011) 2921 7185
E-mail: roli@vsnl.com; Website: rolibooks.com
Also at
Varanasi, Bangalore, Kolkata, Jaipur, Chennai & Mumbai

Cover design: Supriya Saran
Layout design: Narendra Shahi

ISBN: 978-81-7436-530-9
Rs. 250

Typeset in Minion by Roli Books Pvt. Ltd. and
printed at Anubha Printers, Noida.

contents

introduction

Cross-Border Talks is a publishing venture, which seeks to improve understanding between India and Pakistan by inviting eminent Indians and Pakistanis to discuss the issues which divide the two countries within the covers of one book. The series is also distinctive because each volume is published simultaneously in India and Pakistan in order to generate discussion in both countries at the same time.

The first volume in the series, *Diplomatic Divide*, was an analysis of bilateral relations by two senior retired diplomats who had worked with some of the key politicians and witnessed some of the moments of high tension and conflict between Islamabad and Delhi. The second, entitled *Divided by Democracy*, took up an equally important issue – the progress of democracy in the two countries and the factors which have either facilitated or impeded its growth. This third volume, appropriately enough on the sixtieth anniversary of independence, examines the *Fault Lines of Nationhood* and the continuing debate in both countries about what constitutes nationality and how it is construed.

Since 1947, India and Pakistan have had a long and difficult relationship, marred on three occasions by outright war and made potentially much more explosive since 1998 by their possession of the means of mutual destruction. Two of the wars – in 1948 and 1965 – constituted attempts by Pakistan to change the map of South Asia by force and to assert its claim to Kashmir as a former princely state with a Muslim majority. A later war – in 1971 – actually redrew the map, dividing Pakistan, ushering Bangladesh into the community of nations and calling into question the very basis on which a Muslim homeland had been created in 1947.

Such conflicts demonstrated at an early stage that the national boundaries established at Partition were neither universally accepted nor immutable, and even today, despite the much improved state of relations between India and Pakistan, the dispute over Kashmir, whether acknowledged as legitimate or not, is a legacy of Partition which remains a serious impediment to permanent peace.

More broadly, what constitutes nationality or nationhood remains a recurrent topic for debate in both countries. The emergence of Bangladesh as a separate state involved a dramatic recasting of South Asian political geography and was to that extent an exceptional episode. However, the serious divisions within Pakistan over competing claims of religion and ethnicity, which led to the events of 1971, continue to resonate in the new, truncated state, which emerged from that experience. All the smaller Pakistani provinces have witnessed, at one time or another, revolts against the central government, and since the 1980s, even the Mohajirs, who were in the forefront of the movement for Pakistan, have been asserting their claims as a new ethnic minority. Efforts to find a new identity for Pakistan by pursuing policies of Islamisation have also proved highly contested, not least because they have for the most part been imposed by undemocratic regimes.

India has shown much less fragility than Pakistan. As the main successor to the British Raj, it inherited far more effective government machinery and benefited enormously from the long prime ministership of Jawaharlal Nehru, which helped to establish the country as a working democracy. Yet despite its democratic credentials, India's political history has witnessed a number of violent insurgencies against the Central government – most notably in Punjab and Kashmir but also over a longer period in the Northeast. More importantly, since the 1980s, the working of Indian democracy has thrown up important challenges to Nehru's secular political vision. The idea of India as a Hindu nation has gained ground, the Bharatiya Janata Party (BJP) has twice been elected to power at the Centre, albeit in coalition with other parties, and the fears of India's minorities, particularly the Muslims, have palpably increased. While in Pakistan, the issue of Islamisation has provoked intense debate about the basis of nationality and minority rights, in India, the growth of right wing Hindu nationalism has provoked similar heart-searching about India's own political identity.

The authors of *Fault Lines of Nationhood*, Professor Gyanendra Pandey and Dr Yunas Samad, have spent much of their academic lives looking in detail at issues of nationalism and ethnicity in South Asia. Pandey, who teaches at Emory University in the USA, is a leading figure in the subaltern school of Indian history, and has published a number of books on Indian politics. His early work on *The Construction of Communalism in Colonial North India* was followed by more contemporary studies on questions of identity in India. He has also written a book called *Remembering Partition*, which explores issues of violence, nationalism and history. He is currently working on the emergence of Dalit politics in India. Samad, who teaches sociology at Bradford University in the UK, wrote his doctoral thesis on issues of nationalism and ethnicity in Pakistan. Later published as *Nation in Turmoil*, the book broke new ground in straddling independence and examining not only how Muslims were united to demand Pakistan but also how the unity collapsed once Pakistan had been created and the army gradually assumed a key role. More recently, he has made several studies of the process of Islamisation and of political developments among the Mohajirs, who now claim to be Pakistan's fifth nationality.

Pandey begins his essay for this volume by pointing out an important difference between perceptions of nationalism in nineteenth century Europe, where the emphasis was on the unification of nations into single states, and perceptions of nationalism in the twentieth century, in which the dominant theme was the liberation from colonial rule of subject peoples. In this second case, nationalism has been linked very closely with the notion of democracy and equity, though the pressure for homogeneity remains strong and there is often a marked tension between the two dynamics.

Looking at India's own experience of nationalism, Pandey stresses the importance of the concept of majority and minority in the context of the country's increasing democratisation from colonial times onwards. The issue of which community or communities can lay claim to a 'natural' majority and what role is assigned to minorities in any nationalist discourse are central to his understanding of the fault lines of Indian nationhood.

In colonial times, the British rulers saw India as a Hindu country, with a number of religious minorities, some of which were afforded special protection as representative government was introduced. Indian nationalists countered these arguments by stressing the long historical association of all communities with India and by arguing for a common anti-colonial front. With the British decision to partition the country in 1947, however, and the migration of many Muslims to Pakistan, the idea that the Hindus were 'the real Indians' and that the others, particularly the Muslims, 'had to prove that they belonged' was enormously strengthened. Pandey's detailed examination of a Kanpur newspaper editorial of that period provides a valuable psychological insight into the sort of reworking of Indian history, which took place at a popular level at that time.

Such characterisation of Muslims as invaders and aliens may not have been representative. Moreover, in the immediate aftermath of Partition, the leadership of Nehru and the dominance of the Indian National Congress kept such sentiments in political check. They resonate uncannily, however, with the strident arguments put forward forty years later by the BJP, when it mounted its campaign to destroy the Babri Masjid at Ayodhya and rebuild a temple to Ram on the site. As Pandey points out, this later campaign was part of a sustained effort by the BJP and its associates 'to reclaim the national culture from its enemies' and a battle over history – which involved the rewriting of history and of history textbooks – lay at the heart of it. In that particular battle, his own sympathies would undoubtedly lie with those historians of India who were accused by the BJP of un-Indian or Marxist leanings. In his essay, however, he makes an important wider point about such claims to nationhood which is relevant to both Pakistan and India. He argues that all such claims are historically constructed, that they often serve explicit political purposes and that by their very nature they are open to contest.

Pandey then goes on to look at two other communities in India – the Muslims and the Dalits – and the case of the Northeast. In looking at the Muslims, he concentrates largely on the pre-Partition period and the emergence of the demand for Pakistan in the 1940s. Interestingly, both he and Samad agree that Muhammad Ali Jinnah, the leader of the Muslim League, was not intent on Partition but sought a compromise in which Muslim majority states in the north-west and north-east would act as a counterbalance to a Hindu majority state in India. Samad talks about Jinnah working for a 'federation within a confederation' – as was made clear by his acceptance of the Cabinet Mission Plan in 1946. However, Pakistan as a concept remained very vague, perhaps necessarily so, and despite Jinnah's opposition to the partition of Punjab and Bengal, Congress intransigence and communal disorder forced it upon him. Pandey sees the creation of the two new states on the basis of religion as the antithesis of the separation of private and public, which is the essence of what he calls the modern state. This is also an issue which resonates in both countries, where the politicisation of religion has continued to dominate debates about nationhood – whether in India in the 1980s or in Pakistan throughout its history.

The Dalits, formerly known as Untouchables, are an altogether different case. In the early 1930s, under the leadership of Dr Ambedkar, they were on the verge of securing separate representation from the British in the constitutional negotiations of that time. The Congress saw this as a colonial device to divide the Hindu community and Gandhi succeeded in reversing the decision by threatening a fast unto death. Since Independence, however, with the advent of universal suffrage, the abolition of untouchability and the reservation of educational places and jobs for backward communites, the Dalits have gradually emerged as a powerful political force. Pandey highlights the claim of the Bahujan Samaj Party to be the majority of the Indian people – the original inhabitants who were conquered by the Aryan invaders. Here is more reworking of Indian history and much of it highly contestable. What cannot be contested, however, are the benefits which have come to the Dalit community through their acquisition of power via the ballot box. Uttar Pradesh, the country's largest state, has been ruled by a Dalit chief minister on more than one occasion and provides a dramatic example of the way that democracy has gradually worked in favour of this under-privileged community.

Pandey finishes his essay with some reflections on the situation in the north-east of India, where the government has faced tribal insurgencies and charges of internal colonialism, despite its efforts to introduce democratic government and to promote development in this remote region. Concerns about security, a heavy reliance on a military presence and outside contractors are some of the factors, which may have contributed to a sense of alienation. But equally important, he says, is the need for full political participation, for social justice and respect for cultural difference, which are vital elements of an effective working democracy.

Samad's analysis of Pakistani nationalism and its antecedents follows a remarkably similar trajectory. He begins by looking at two essentialist perspectives. The first is the two-nation theory, which argues that the Muslim community in India always was identifiably separate. The second is the Marxist theory of nationalism, which equates nationality with language. He finds neither satisfactory. With Benedict Anderson and others, he argues that identity is not fixed or inflexible but contingent and fluid. Identities can be imagined and re-imagined, just as histories can be written and re-written, and memories revived or erased. In fact, Samad shows very clearly in his essay how the history of Pakistani nationalism has often involved the erasure of memory – whether after 1947, when the hybridity of the Muslim experience in India was conveniently forgotten, or after 1971, when the Bengali dimension of Pakistani nationalism was airbrushed from the history books.

Another important tool used by Samad in interpreting Pakistani nationalism is one developed by Hamza Alavi, the Pakistani scholar to whose memory this volume is dedicated. Hamza Alavi argued that identity politics in Pakistan has been driven by pressure from class interests, which mobilise support around specific cultural or language agendas with a view to accessing employment opportunities within the state structure. He coined the term 'salariat' to describe this phenomenon, which has been particularly important in Pakistan because of the dominance of the state in the employment market. Samad traces the growth of Muslim nationalism in India before Independence and the various conflicts afterwards between the centre and the provinces in terms of competition for state resources between different 'salariats'. In India, before Partition, the Muslim League drew support from those who feared they would be at a disadvantage in a united India and opted for new opportunities in Pakistan. After 1947, the Pakistani state was dominated by Urdu speakers – Punjabis and Mohajirs particularly – who were resistant to the claims of the Bengali speaking 'salariat' for fair access to jobs and other state resources. Many of these conflicts revolve around issues of language and which languages are privileged by the state. In that sense they are not just about jobs but about how education is organised and which languages are prescribed.

Yunas Samad also focuses on the role and character of the state, which he sees as central to the way in which challenges to the status quo are managed. In contrast to Pandey's understanding of Indian nationalism as a twentieth century phenomenon – with strong links to democracy – he believes that the Pakistani state has adopted a more nineteenth century approach to nationalism and has been keener on eliminating difference than on managing it by negotiation. In fact, though Pandey points to the dangers of internal colonialism in some parts of India, Samad argues that this phenomenon has been more or less endemic in Pakistan, and that on the whole India has been more successful in accommodating differences through the working of its federal system.

After an introduction on theories of nationalism, Yunas Samad divides the rest of his essay into three parts. The first deals with the rise of Muslim nationalism in India and the demand for Pakistan. The second looks at the emergence of Bangladesh. The third examines the growth of Islamic nationalism from the 1980s onwards and the emergence of a new Mohajir ethnicity in the cities of Sindh.

In his examination of Muslim nationalism, Samad traces the development of the Muslim salariat from the time of Sir Seyed Ahmed Khan onwards. He shows how colonial language policy, the introduction of representative institutions, and an increasing sense of vulnerability in the Muslim minority provinces as provincial autonomy was introduced gave rise to the demand for Pakistan, which was first voiced by the Muslim League in 1940. He describes the Muslim League platform as a 'minority rights discourse', which involved stigmatising the Congress as a Hindu party, which was riding roughshod over Muslim rights where it was in power. He also emphasises, however, the real difficulty of uniting a highly disparate and divided community and he argues that Mr Jinnah's refusal to define what he meant by Pakistan was because he knew very well that 'it would have opened up the very same fault lines which were to appear once Pakistan was established'.

Looking at post-Partition Pakistan politics, Yunas Samad argues that the rulers of the new state abandoned the minority rights discourse almost as soon as they came to power. Before Partition there had been virtual unanimity among Muslim groups on the importance of decentralisation and provincial autonomy – for fear of Congress dominance of the central government – but afterwards, Pakistan's new rulers were to lay their emphasis on the importance of strong central government and to prove highly resistant to demands for real autonomy in the provinces, whether in East Pakistan or elsewhere.

Samad looks in some detail at the reasons why Pakistan failed to accommodate the Bengali salariat in the first two decades after Independence. He explains the reluctance of Jinnah and his successors to recognise the Bengali language in terms of the virtual monopoly of power enjoyed by the Urdu-speaking salariat – chiefly the Punjabis and Mohajirs who dominated the civil service and the army. This resulted in a fragmentation of the Pakistani salariat, the emergence of a powerful Bengali political movement and ultimately to the division of the country.

Once Bangladesh had broken away, the scene was set for the Punjabis to increase their dominance of the state. This derives not just from the fact that numerically they constitute a substantial majority of the population but also because of their entrenched position in the civil service and the army. Yunas Samad points out that the Punjabis do not need to stress their ethnic identity because they have willingly embraced the larger Pakistani identity and are benefiting from their association with the state. It is an interesting parallel to Pandey's point that Hindus in India do not feel the need to qualify their nationality. Both communities claim to constitute some sort of 'natural' majority to which other minority communities must relate, though for that very reason, their claim to pre-eminence needs to be questioned.

In parallel with this development, Pakistan embarked upon a programme of Islamisation, which Samad sees as an attempt to provide justification and respectability for the military regime of General Zia ul Haq. The first steps had been taken earlier under the flawed democratic leadership of Zulfiquar Ali Bhutto. Under Zia ul Haq, however, the introduction of punitive punishments, the levying and distribution of Islamic taxes and the development of a vast new unregulated Islamic educational sector were to have more far-reaching effects on the country's politics. The experience of growing sectarianism and discrimination against women, which these conservative policies have unleashed, has provoked a backlash among liberal Pakistanis, who make the point that the country's founder had absolutely no sympathy with ideas of theocratic government. As a result of these policies, however, and growing popular opposition to developments in

Iraq and the wider Middle East, the *ulama* in Pakistan are now a more powerful political force than ever before, particularly in the north of the country, and Islamic nationalism has a growing appeal.

The emergence of the Mohajirs as a new nationality was in some ways the obverse side of the coin of growing Punjabi dominance. In the early days of Pakistan, the Mohajirs had been important players in the structure of politics, government and the military, but after the Soviet intervention in Afghanistan, when Pakistan became centrally involved in supporting the Afghan resistance, they were gradually displaced by the Pakhtuns in the civil-military oligarchy which ruled the country under General Zia ul Haq. In the 1970s, the Mohajirs, as a relatively well educated community settled in the urban areas of Sindh, had already begun to feel the pinch as Sindhi politicians campaigned for greater recognition of their language and greater access to government jobs. In the 1980s, however, Samad shows how they re-invented themselves as new ethnic minority and became a powerful political force in Sindh seeking remedy both through the ballot box and by militant action for their increasing sense of deprivation.

Samad concludes his analysis with the reflection that persistent authoritarian rule has made it much more difficult to solve the country's serious ethnic problems. What is required, he argues, is a deepening of the democratic process, so that, as has happened in India, the ballot box can provide real opportunities for the transfer of resources to excluded and marginalised communities. Here Samad and Pandey are in agreement on the importance of full political participation if there is to be any chance of establishing some degree of social, cultural and economic equity. In Pakistan's case, however, the fact that the armed forces take so large a slice of the budget leaves very little for real development, with or without democracy. For much of

Pakistan's history, defence against India has been given the highest priority and has justified the country's highly skewed budgets. Yunas Samad points to the urgent need, therefore, for an improvement in relations between the two countries, so that the human needs of their growing populations can be more readily met.

David Page
July 2007

india: mainstreams and minorities

gyanendra pandey

there is a fundamental connection between nationalism and democracy that has not, to my mind, been grasped as clearly as it should be. I think it will be widely acknowledged that the power of the national idea comes from the link between people and nation: the history and culture, the unity and independence, the politics, the interests, of the people/nation. Equally the fault lines of nationhood are to be found, as many scholars have begun to note, in the very insistence on the idea of a unified, homogenised people/nation. The implications of these observations need to be teased out a little more than they have been in the past.

It is commonly said that the aim of all nationalists is to bring about a convergence between the national population and the territory of governance: one culture, one people, one nation and one state. Obviously what remains under-theorised in such a proposition is how the nation, people, culture in question comes into being as a unified nation, people or culture in the first place. This is precisely the question that scholars from Elie Kedourie and Anthony Smith to Ernest Gellner, Eric Hobsbawm, Benedict Anderson and Partha Chatterjee have sought to investigate.[1] What also remains insufficiently realised is the extent of variation in the conditions under which such peoples and nations are constituted, and the terms on which – or perhaps one should say, the units in which – they come together. These contracting units are rarely, if ever, those of the individual and the state alone. Individuals and states emerge out of histories that produce social formations and social assemblages of many kinds: and neither individual nor state is at liberty to neglect these pre-existing groupings altogether. I shall have more to say about this presently.

In relation to nationalism, let me point out first what seems to me to be an important difference between the experience of the nineteenth and the twentieth centuries. A primary feature of nationalisms in the twentieth century, which distinguishes them from the more commonly cited examples (or 'models') of the nineteenth, is that they took the form of struggles for liberation. If the unification of nations into single states (one language, one culture, one people, one nation) was the goal of European nationalisms in the nineteenth century, the liberation of subject peoples was the characteristic mark of the nationalisms of the twentieth century. The nationalist movements of the period have been recognised as being part of a widespread anti-colonial and anti-imperialist struggle; but they took on other dimensions as well – as may be seen in the struggle against fascist, autocratic rule in Spain and against warlords (many of whom collaborated with Western powers) in China. Central to the liberation struggles of the twentieth century was a call to stop the exploitation of 'man' by 'man', to put an end to the privilege of birth and the dominance of inherited race, caste, class and gender power, and to bring this about through the institution of structures of political equality, social justice and economic advancement. It is this shared aspiration that allowed Jawaharlal Nehru to say, in 1939, that the frontiers of the Indian national movement lay in China in the east and Spain in the west.

The struggle for equality was of course implicit in numerous political movements of the nineteenth century, and explicit in the revolutionary struggles of the late eighteenth century, in France, North America and Haiti. There is no clear consensus among scholars about the extent to which these revolutionary struggles might be described as nationalist. Even if they are, however, it is evident that developments in the twentieth century served in several important ways to deepen and concretise the goals of liberty, equality and fraternity. Thus, the years of what is called the First World War helped to throw up not only the slogan of the right of nations to self-determination, but also the ideals of the Bolshevik Revolution – a state of society in which the poorest and most downtrodden would compete on equal terms with the high-born and the privileged, in which indeed privilege associated with birth would no longer survive. The agitations and campaigns of working class and women's groups had already, before this, given considerable legitimacy to the idea of adult franchise (even though it was to be a long time still before governments elected by *all* the people, irrespective of income, education, occupation, gender, race, religious affiliation and the like, would become the norm – even in Europe). The Russian workers' and peasants' and subaltern soldiers' demand for Peace, Land and Bread helped to spell out the needs and conditions of modern democracy in other directions.

It is ironical, but not altogether surprising, that the idea of universal voting rights for all the inhabitants of a politically unified territory, including women and other historically underprivileged groups, was instituted in a country like India some time before it was accepted in every part of Europe and North America. Nor is it strange that the Indian national struggle for liberation from colonial rule was already being articulated in the 1930s and 1940s in terms of the need to dismantle the economic, social and cultural structures of colonialism, along with the political writ of the white man. The call for the abolition of *zamindari* (landlordism) and the institution of a socialist ethos, if not a socialist society, was very much a part of the national demand in this last phase of struggle against British rule.

When, at one point in the 1920s, Mohandas Karamchand Gandhi articulated the goal of 'truthful relations between Hindus and Musalmans, bread for the masses and removal of untouchability' as his definition of *swaraj* (self-rule), he was enunciating a sense of national independence that was fundamentally at variance with the nineteenth century European conception of one language, one culture, often one religion, and, therefore, one nation. It was, at the same time, a conception of the future political community that was not less radical than the Bolsheviks' slogan of Peace, Land and Bread, even if it was expressed in very different, Gandhian terms.

What I am arguing is that nationalism in the twentieth century is inextricably linked with the notion of democracy, although it continues to be overdetermined by nineteenth century European notions of a homogenised people, culture, history and nation-state. This latter-day nationalism, which I submit is the predominant form of nationalism as we know it, has always been caught between the two discourses – that of the homogeneous people, nation, culture, on the one hand, and that of democracy and equity on the other. It has never resolved, perhaps can never resolve the competing demands of the two. For while the notion of the unified nation/people has repeatedly brought forth the claim of ancient, or at any rate essential, oneness and commonality, the requirements of democracy have necessitated attention to inherited inequalities and disabilities – of gender, caste, class, race, religion, region. They have also necessitated an analysis of societies in terms of majorities and minorities, a reckoning undertaken not only through the counting of heads in the expression of opinions or choice on particular issues, but also by the distribution of inherited characteristics – precisely those matters that tend to divide the nation – on the basis of affirmed language, race, religion, region, caste or class.

Twentieth century nationalisms have had to contend from the very beginning with the issue of majorities and minorities. The claim of the homogeneous nation demanding its own state turns out in most cases to be the claim of a putative 'mainstream' or 'majority' that lives on more or less agreed terms, and almost inescapably in a state of some tension, with a variety of historically constituted minorities. The point about the historical constitution, and political affirmation, of majority or minority status is of importance, for it signals at once that there is nothing automatic or inevitable about these statuses – either as claim or as ascription. Yet there are significant differences between the positions of self-proclaimed majorities and minorities.

The majority, as a political category, is often invisible, even though it remains contestable. The political invisibility of the majority derives from a claim to a *natural* equivalence with the (pre-existing) nation. Unlike a minority, the majority can therefore proceed as though it does not need to be named except in national terms, as the nation. The 'majority' becomes the unmarked national – Indian, American, Australian, Chinese; not Hindu Indian, White Anglo-Saxon Protestant American, White Australian, or Han Chinese. The 'minority' becomes the hyphenated or marked citizen – Indian Muslims or Christians, Chinese Muslims, African or Hispanic Americans, and even (incredibly) native Americans and indigenous Australians.

Claims of 'majority' status come to be established usually through the cultural, economic and political power of those who articulate the majority position. It is sometimes reinforced – or even initiated – by the way in which colonial and other autocratic regimes have distributed and governed the subject population. And it is often confirmed by those seeking protection as 'minorities' in existing or proposed political arrangements in a given territory. However, such attributions of 'majority' and 'minority' also come to be established as part of a popular common sense over a longer period, through the circulation of historical accounts, such as the history of 'Hindu', 'Muslim' and 'British' rule in the Indian subcontinent; the classification of populations (in censuses, electoral registers and other documentation) as Hindu, Muslim, Sikh, Anglo-Indian, etc; and of course through ongoing conflicts for jobs, education, and more general political and social advantage, between groups increasingly designated in these terms.

Colonial India was seen by its British rulers as a Hindu country. The Muslims, the Sikhs, the Christians, the Parsis and others were seen, and in most cases came to see themselves, as so many minorities, likely to be at the receiving end in an independent Indian state based on standard principles of representative government. The nationalist response to this kind of construction was the proposition that India was made up of several communities, all very much part of the land because of their long historical association with it: Hindu + Muslim + Christian + Parsi + Sikh. However, the proposition about a majority religious community living alongside a number of minority ones remained in place. This classification, and this sense of *permanent* advantage or disadvantage, is what the diverse political claims of Hindus, Muslims, Sikhs and others on the eve of Partition and Independence were about.

I am suggesting that the articulation of majority and minority positions is very much a part of nationalist discourse, not outside of or pursuant to it. The majority – or a 'majority' – articulates itself as the *real* nation, to which other groups, elements, assemblages are (or have been) added. These additional elements may be represented as having enriched the nation, given it depth, variety, colour, new tastes, new foods, new scientific and artistic and philosophical potential. They remain, however, in the nationalist discourse, *additions, enrichments* of a core that somehow, already always exists. The Indian example provides a very good illustration. Indian nationalists have long promoted the idea of 'unity in diversity': the long coexistence of many of the world's great religions, the multitude of languages and cultures that went to make up the rich tapestry and wisdom of Indian civilisation. At the same time, this proposition has coexisted with notions of *tolerance* and *assimilation*. The question that is not asked is: tolerance *of whom*, and assimilation *by whom*?

On the one hand, then, we have the notion of layer upon layer of settlement, and the mingling of cultures and traditions to produce a higher synthesis – the poet's '*karavaan baste gaye, Hindostan banta gaya*' (caravans of travellers came and settled on these lands, and India came to be). On the other, India (Hindustan) is, in some curious and unexplained way, always already present, even before the coming of the first caravans, one might say. As Nehru put it, 'Some kind of a dream of unity has occupied the mind of India since the dawn of civilisation... Some powerful impulse, some tremendous urge, or idea of the significance of life ... was impressed upon the subconscious mind of India when she was fresh and young at the very dawn of history.' Or Lajpat Rai: 'India is not Hindu or Muslim. It is not even both. It is one. It is India.'[2]

I shall spell out this 'majority' nationalist position in the second section of this essay, in which I also make the point that, in India as elsewhere, the putative 'majority' has sometimes felt that it has been denied the cultural or ideological power – the dominance – that it believes to be its right. Such is the case with white supremacists in Europe, as well as the Hindu majority in India since the 1980s. In later sections, I take up the politics of two very different kinds of minorities in the subcontinent – the Muslims and the Dalits (Scheduled Castes or ex-Untouchables).

I shall suggest that there are two stages in the politics of a 'minority'. One, which is sometimes overlooked, is a struggle to gain recognition as a minority: that is to say, as a legal/political category with a legal/political recognition of group rights. This is dramatically illustrated in the case of the Dalits, a 'minority' that never quite gains the status of a constitutionally recognised minority but cannot be denied some of the protection and special rights that may be claimed by one.

The second stage, or aspect, of minority politics is the struggle to maintain or, if possible, extend its rights as a minority. This is an exercise that Muslims and Dalits, along with other minority groups in India, have long been engaged in – of course with varying results. Here the task for 'nationalism', or for the majority that claims the nationalist position and concedes (or asserts) the minority status of other groups in the society, is to prevent a minority discourse from developing into an argument about internal colonialism, in which the relations between majority and minority are seen, once more, as a relationship of colonial domination, and the political resolution of the problem is seen in a political separation or partition.

Dalits and Muslims are, of course, not the only marginalised or subordinated groups that have made an argument about being unequal citizens, discriminated against in what is officially supposed to be their own land. There are other kinds of 'minorities', or more precisely other kinds of sectional demands and movements that need to be taken up in an examination of the fault lines of nationhood in India. The separatist claims of political groups in Kashmir, Punjab and the Northeast are perhaps the most commonly cited examples of these. I shall conclude, therefore, with a brief discussion of the imbroglio in the Northeast, which is rather less well known than either the Kashmir or the Punjab case. I shall question what 'majority' and 'minority', and democracy, and the charge of internal colonialism, mean in this context.

I submit that there is something about the overriding claims of the nation-state, and about its naturalness and sanctity that works to undermine many moves towards acceptable political resolutions in situations of conflict. What is denied in the reigning discourse of nationalism is the historical character of all claims to nationhood, national rights and national belonging. Yet it is precisely because of the historically constructed character of claims, or attributions, of natural belonging (or not belonging), of national or anti-national conduct, and of majority and minority status that they remain open to contest, and are often contested.

This essay on the fault lines of Indian nationhood is about that contest, about the making of such claims in the history of nationalism in the subcontinent, and about some of the unforeseen implications of the historical articulation of particular national boundaries (geographical, cultural and political) and of particular majority and minority positions. What I seek to examine is how a number of different social and political assemblages in India have deployed these ideas of majority and minority, belonging and not belonging, or alternatively responded to the claims or charges contained in them.

whose country is it anyway?

Let us begin with the nationalist categorisation of friends and enemies as it is encountered in India immediately after the establishment of an independent Indian state in August 1947. Given the circumstances accompanying this Independence, notably the division of British India into the two successor states of India and Pakistan, the common construction of 'us' and 'them' in the newly independent nation served to reinforce a conceptual split between the Hindu/Indian, on the one hand, and the Muslim/foreigner, on the other. The easy, indeed un-stated, assumption that the Hindus were the real Indians, and that other communities – especially the Muslims – had to prove that they belonged, is found in all manner of nationalist statements at this time. The vernacular press speaking for the non-metropolitan intelligentsia – provincial notables, small town professionals, teachers, journalists, traders and clerks, who lent a great deal of the most vocal support to the nationalism of this period – provides any number of examples.

It will perhaps suffice if I cite just one, from an editorial in the Hindi daily, *Vartman*, published from Kanpur in the state of Uttar Pradesh (or U.P.) on 12 October 1947. The editorial asks the question 'Whose country is this?' in its first line. The answer is provided at once: 'All those who can call India their native land [*swadesh*] in the real sense of the term, this country is theirs.' The editors then proceed to spell out how the Buddhists and Jains, Sikhs, Christians, Anglo-Indians, and Parsis all belong here, because they think of India as their native land. Persecuted in early times, some Hindus became Buddhists and Jains. 'However, they did not change their nationality [*sic*]. They did not leave the country. They did not start calling themselves Chinese or Japanese.' Similarly, a Sikh *panth* (community or tradition) arose. 'This Sikh community also recognises India as their *janmabhumi* [land of their birth] and therefore their country.'[3]

The analysis so far is simple. The Buddhists (even though they had practically disappeared from the land of the Buddha), Jains, and Sikhs treated India as the land of their birth because this is where they and their religious traditions were born. They are, in that sense 'original', 'natural' Indians, The argument in the case of the other small religious (and racial) groupings – the Christians, Anglo-Indians, and Parsis – is not quite so straightforward. Many of the lowest castes and classes had embraced Christianity in recent times, the editorial noted, to escape the worst oppression of untouchability, as much as anything else. 'Yet they did not forget that they could never go and settle in Europe; [they knew that] India would always be their country.'

The Anglo-Indians had, on the other hand, remained ambivalent for some time. They were after all Eurasian, both English and Indian by blood, and many of them had sought to migrate (as they would continue to do during the 1950s, and to some extent later). But there were two points which went in their favour, as *Vartman* saw it. First, their numbers were never very great; they would never constitute a demographic threat to the nation. Secondly, the departing British had left them to fend for themselves: 'they came to their senses as soon as the British left' and recognised India as their native land.

The propositions here are patronising, and full of paradoxes. The Indian Christians could not dream of settling in Europe. The Anglo-Indians did dream of it, but were left high and dry by the departing colonial rulers. In any case, the two communities were numerically small and very widely dispersed. They had no other country to go to, and they constituted no threat to 'the nation' or its culture. India could therefore be treated as their native land.

The argument was different again in the case of the Parsis. They came to the country from Iran, not as aggressors or missionaries, it is said, but as refugees, fleeing to save their lives (although one might note that some of them came as traders too). Nor did they give up their religion, culture, or language on settling here. 'Nevertheless, many of them have contributed to the economic, intellectual, social, and political development of India like true citizens.' This is a line of reasoning with which we are not unfamiliar. Wealthy Japanese entrepreneurs, Arab sheikhs and Indian computer whiz kids are welcome in the United States,

Britain and Australia because they contribute to the 'economic' and 'intellectual' development of these areas: not so the Bradford Muslims or Sikhs of Southall, Mexican and Cuban casual labourers or Vietnamese boat-people. This was what went in favour of the Parsis in India, apart from the fact that they were a small, almost microscopic minority. Due to the fairly privileged economic and social position they enjoyed in places like Bombay, many of them had – 'like true citizens' – contributed to the economic, intellectual, social, and political development of India.

The case of the Muslims of the subcontinent was another matter altogether. Conversions to Islam had taken place on a very large scale, so that there were by the 1940s ninety million Muslims in the land, 25 per cent of the total population of undivided India. A large number of these Muslims had come from the depressed classes of the Hindu population, the paper acknowledged: they had become Muslims to escape from the extreme sanctions and disabilities of the caste system. However, resisting the oppressiveness of the Hindu caste system was one thing; shedding one's 'national' culture, religion, language, and dress another. 'Flesh and blood of the Hindus though they were, these Hindavi Muslims came to think of themselves as belonging to the Arab and Mughal communities [or nations: the term *jati* can refer to either]... Rulers like Aurangzeb, and later on the British, never tired of preaching that they [the Muslims] have been the governors of this country, and that their direct links are with Arabia, Persia, and Turkey. Their language, appearance, religion, and practices are all different from those of the Hindus.'

The *Vartman* editorial refers to the tyranny and destructiveness of the Muslim invaders. It adds that the local converts have been even more tyrannical and destructive, attacking Hindu temples, images and religious processions and making a point of sacrificing the cow at the *Baqr Id*, precisely because the cow was sacred to the Hindus. These sweeping and astonishing generalisations, however, are by way of rhetorical flourish: 'well known' propositions (as we are told) that serve only to underline the basic argument that the Muslims of India are, or may be suspected of being, alien because 'when they changed their religion, they also dreamt up schemes of changing their country.' 'They did not think of the [other] people living in India as their own. They thought of the local language [as if there were only one!] as foreign. They cut themselves off from Indian civilisation and culture.'

In the course of the anti-colonial struggle, the argument goes on, when people of every other community joined in a common fight for freedom, the Muslims stood in the way. They made separatist demands, played into the hands of the British, and were rewarded, finally, with the prize of Pakistan – from where Hindus were now being driven out. Many Indian Muslims had earlier tried to migrate to Persia, Arabia, Mesopotamia, and Turkey, only to return disappointed. Today, 'if there was place in Pakistan, if there were agricultural lands, jobs, and if they had their way, [these Muslims] would undoubtedly go and settle there.' On other occasions, the editors of *Vartman* had declared that all Indian Muslims viewed Pakistan as their Mecca, and Jinnah as their modern Prophet.

Now, on 12 October 1947, the editorial continued: large numbers of Muslims had already gone to settle in Pakistan, and many more sat waiting to go. As for the rest, who had decided to stay back, did they show signs of willingness to live in peace with the other communities of India – 'Sikh, Jain, Buddhists, Christians, Parsis and Anglo-Indians?' 'These machine-guns, mortars, rifles, pistols, bombs, dynamite, swords, spears and daggers, that are being discovered daily [in Muslim houses and localities], are all these being collected for the defence of India?' The problem, according to the editorial, was that there was just not enough place for all of these Muslims in Pakistan. However, the fact that so many stayed on in India was no reason to think of them automatically as Indian. There was need for greater discrimination than that.

It would perhaps be a waste of time to point out all the errors of fact and the blatant half-truths that pepper *Vartman's* analysis of the Muslim condition.[4] There is one feature of the statement, however, that requires special emphasis. At some stage in this articulation of the conditions of citizenship, an argument about culture gives way almost imperceptibly to an argument about politics – or, more precisely, about political power. The Anglo-Indians, unable to attain the numerical strength of the Muslims, never constituted a threat. The Parsis remained different in religion, culture and 'language', as the Hindi newspaper had it, but they had contributed significantly to 'our' political, economic, intellectual, and social development. The Muslims had, on the other hand, put forward their own, separatist demands, and had stood in the way of the united struggle against the British. They had not accepted 'our' concept of India: they were therefore not Indians.

There is another important aspect of this articulation. It is noteworthy that in the entire analysis, the Hindus appear only a couple of times, in passing, as the people from whom the Muslims sought to differentiate themselves. An editorial that elaborates the character and place of the different religious communities of India in answer to the question 'Whose country is this?' does not even feel the need to mention the Hindu community as a separate constituent of the nation. For the Hindus are not a constituent. They *are* the nation, the 'we' who demand cooperation from the minorities, the 'us' that the Muslims have to learn to live with. Like the land and the trees, the rivers and mountains, these invisible Hindus are the nation's natural condition, its essence and spirit. Their culture is the nation's culture, their history its history. This needs no demonstration, or for that matter even declaration.

There was a poignant moment in the Indian Constituent Assembly debates on the question of minority rights when Frank Anthony, the Anglo-Indian leader, referred to a comment sometimes made to him that he should drop the prefix 'Anglo' from his description of his community if he was as strongly committed to India as he claimed. Anthony's response was that, 'good or bad', 'right or wrong', the word 'Anglo-Indian' 'connotes to me many things which I hold dear'. He went further, however: 'I will drop it readily, as soon as you drop your label... The day you drop the label of "Hindu", the day you forget that you are a Hindu, that day – no, two days before that – I will drop by deed poll, by beat of drum if necessary, the prefix "Anglo". That day, he added, 'will be welcome first and foremost to the minorities of India.'[5]

The Anglo-Indian leader's argument was logical, but misplaced. It would have appeared meaningless to many Hindus, who did not have to use the designation 'Hindu' in any case. At Partition and for a long time afterwards, they were the silent, invisible majority. They did not need to advertise the fact that they were Hindus. For some time after the assassination of Gandhi by a Hindu extremist, it was even a little difficult for the more militant among them to do so. In as much as they were Hindu, they were automatically Indian. It was enough in this age of high nationalism to claim the latter designation. The question of what it meant to be a Hindu, what advantages such a classification brought to the lower castes and classes, and whether the Hindus as a whole were underprivileged, was not to be taken up in a sustained way until the 1980s and '90s.[6]

To have given greater political visibility to the category of 'Hindu' at the moment of nationalist triumph in the 1940s would perhaps have meant running the risk of differentiating and problematising it, and having to recognise that history, culture and 'naturalness' are not uncontested. This may also be the reason why the argument about whose country India was could not be acknowledged as a *political* argument. To concede that the nation was a political project, first and foremost, would be to concede its historicity. To acknowledge that the nationalist struggle was a struggle for political power would be to open up the question of who should wield that power and to what end – for the progress of the nation could not mean exactly the same thing to all parts of that imagined community.

There was a tacit agreement (as it seemed) that, while these political questions would have to be tackled in the constitution-making body and elsewhere, they must be kept separate from the 'sacred and natural' history of nationalism. This set of questions remained suspended, therefore, in the course of the nationalist debates at the time of Partition and Independence. Thus, a particular articulation of nationhood emerged, in which the Muslims had an unenviable place, the Dalits and other oppressed castes and classes were unseen or only symbolically present (as the 'backward' parts of the nation, to be lifted up by those who ruled in the 'general interest,' for the advancement of the nation as a whole), and other religious minorities and marginal nationalities had to work in collaboration with, and willy-nilly in subordination to, that other invisible category, 'the mainstream, Hindu majority.'

I mentioned the 1980s and '90s a moment ago. These decades saw the curious emergence of a powerful right wing Hindu movement in India, now demanding the preservation of the rights of the 'Hindus' as an aggrieved 'minority'. This new Hindu assertiveness was built around an aggressive restatement about the *truth* of a national culture and a national monument. The culture in question is the culture of a Hindu India, the monument a disused sixteenth-century mosque in Ayodhya, a small town in the north Indian province of Uttar Pradesh. Between 1986 and 1992, when the mosque was torn down by a huge gathering of Hindu militants, yelling victory to their gods and their nation, the Babri Masjid in Ayodhya ('Babar's Mosque', allegedly built at the instance of the first Mughal king in 1528) was the symbolic centre of a movement to 'liberate' India by liberating the claimed birthplace of the popular deity, Ram, which was said to be at the precise spot occupied by the mosque.

The battle over the site has become quieter since then, but it has hardly concluded. The issue continues to fester, and comes to the fore periodically, threatening to set off (or actually, as in Gujarat in early 2002, becoming the occasion for) new rounds of open violence against Muslims. The tension increases whenever the date approaches for a crucial hearing or pronouncement in the long-running court cases regarding the disputed site, but also it seems in the run-up to closely fought elections. Looming over all this is the question of what constitutes the national culture, how this is to be defined, and by whom.

The conflict over the Babri Masjid in Ayodhya is part of a larger right-wing Hindu political project to reclaim the 'national culture' from its enemies – Muslims, but also secularists and Westernisers. This war over culture has been waged at numerous sites in recent years – in the cinema, where nudity and lesbianism (and other professedly 'non-Indian' practices) are not to be portrayed; in modern art, where a renowned Muslim painter has been targeted for his representation of the goddess of learning, Saraswati, in semi-clad condition (although Hindu goddesses have been represented nude or semi-nude in temple sculpture and cave paintings for a millennium);[7] in educational institutions, on public buses and on the streets, where women have on occasion been attacked for dressing in jeans and skirts, or deporting themselves in other 'Western' (that is to say, 'untraditional') ways; in history text-books, the writers of which are asked to underline the great achievements of the Hindu past, and to recognise 'the indigenous origins of the Aryans' (i.e., that the Hindus, unlike Muslim, Christian and other alleged 'migrants', always belonged to this land); and so on.

This renewed attempt by the Hindu right to reclaim the cultural and ideological centre of India was provoked by changes in the electoral situation and attempts by left-wing and lower-caste parties to redefine the political nation and to forge a new alliance capable of delivering victory at the polls. With the collapse of the old Brahman/Dalit/Muslim (upper-caste/untouchable/minority) combination that had long served as the ground for the Congress's repeated electoral successes, social democratic parties of leftist inclination sought to build a rainbow coalition of lower castes and minorities (who, together with the Dalits or ex-Untouchables, add up to an overwhelming majority of the population) around an increasingly prosperous and politically assertive group of rich peasant castes.

In response, a more conservative and upper-caste right wing turned to a re-building of the nation in a more pronounced Hindu mould. This was represented by the leading Hindu political party, the Bharatiya Janata Party (BJP), and associated cultural and political organizations, such as the Rashtriya Svayam Sevak Sangh (or RSS), the Vishwa Hindu Parishad (or 'World Hindu Council', VHP), and the Bombay-based Shiv Sena. Many of these organisations had well-organised militias or storm-troopers, which played a leading part in the assault on the Babri Masjid and on other 'anti-national' cultural symbols. This Hindu movement benefited from the open or tacit support of elements of the old Congress party, including several Congress governments in the 1980s and '90s, in part motivated by the same kind of electoral calculations.

Much of the struggle over new political constituencies and

the definition of the *real* India has taken the form of a struggle over history. The resurgent Hindu movement of the last twenty years has actively advanced what it sees as a new, alternative history of India, one that is said to be in tune with the unique character and traditions of its people. Its historians have warned against 'distorted' and 'un-Indian' interpretations of the past served up by 'pseudo-secularist' historians. The accusation against 'pseudo-secularists' is an intriguing one, for it charges them (Marxists, socialists, social democrats, liberals who oppose the attempted Hinduisation of state practices and public culture in India) of having departed from a 'true' secularism, and claims the latter as the position embraced by the Hindus and Hindu parties. It makes this claim on the basis of a fundamental Hindu belief in non-violence, tolerance and coexistence, even as it asserts that 'secularism', like Marxism, socialism, nudity and so on are Western exports to India.

The battle over the content of the national culture and traditions is manifestly unfinished. The chief sufferers of the renewed public contest over issues of secularism, religious heritage and culture however, have not been 'pseudo-secularist' or Marxist intellectuals, or other members of the privileged and Westernized middle classes, but far more ordinary and unprivileged members of the Muslim and other minority communities. Let me turn to the case of the Muslims now.

muslim claims

In the eyes of advocates of a composite Indian nationalism, led by the Indian National Congress, communalism (which here refers to a condition of suspicion, fear and conflict between people belonging to different religious denominations) had in the years after the First World War become the most important political problem to be overcome in the struggle against British colonialism. As far back as 1928, the Nehru Report – the product

of a multi-party conference called to discuss the outlines of a
future constitution for India – declared that 'the communal
problem ... is primarily the Hindu-Muslim problem.'[8]

Different political groups of course saw the problem
differently. For many colonialist administrators and observers,
Hindu-Muslim differences signalled not a 'communal' but an
'international' problem. As Theodore Morison put it in 1932, 'It is
useless to enumerate the grounds of difference between Hindu
and Muslim; the only thing that matters is that they do in fact feel
and think of themselves as separate peoples. In all disquisitions
on nationality this is the only test which is found to cover all
cases.... Judged by this standard the Muslims of India are a
nation. Communal differences, as they are called, are really
national jealousies.'[9] The question for us is how the Muslim
minority and those who claimed to represent it formulated their
concerns.

A critical moment here is Partition. The articulation of the
demand for partition by the leaders of the Muslim League allows
us to analyse something of what was called the Hindu-Muslim
problem. The years 1945 to 1947 were marked by intense struggle
in the subcontinent. What the Second World War established, and
the end of the war underlined, was the changed military, political
and economic position of Britain in the world, and the radical
transformation of the political temper in India. All this lent
unprecedented urgency to the question of the transfer of power
and the establishment of national government(s) in the
subcontinent. It was in this situation that the Congress
leadership, jailed for threatening to launch another campaign of
civil disobedience against the British, was released, efforts at
mobilisation of different sections of the society were actively
renewed, large-scale urban demonstrations and rural uprisings
occurred, new elections were held, and sustained high-level
constitutional negotiations were resumed after 1945.

Much of the politics of the previous three or four decades had been about national liberation. It was a serious complication that the call for Indian self-government was now joined by the call for Muslim self-government in a new country to be named Pakistan. Talk of independence was rife. However, while the Congress and those in sympathy with it expected the independence of a united India, the Muslim League slogan became 'Pakistan for Independence'. There were two nations in India, it was argued, and the acceptance of the Pakistan demand was the only road to the genuine independence of all Indians, the Muslims in a free Pakistan and the Hindus in a free Hindustan.

Yet the idea of 'Pakistan' itself, the proposal for a partition of British India between its Muslim-majority and its Hindu-majority provinces, had not had a long history. It was in March 1940 that the Muslim League formally proposed the establishment of separate 'states' for the Muslim-majority regions of north-western and north-eastern India;[10] and as late as September 1944, in his correspondence with Gandhi, and April 1946, in a meeting of all Muslim League legislators of the centre and the provinces, Jinnah and the Muslim League were still having to clarify that the proposal was for *one* sovereign, independent state called Pakistan (with its separate, eastern and western, wings).

I have argued elsewhere that the Muslim League demand for Pakistan from 1940 onwards was in its essentials a demand for the protection of the place and culture of the Muslims in any future political arrangement. In its clearest expositions, and for most of the period 1940-47, what this envisaged was the autonomy, or independence, of Muslim-majority regions in the north-west and north-east of India – a land (or lands?) where Muslims, and therefore the ideals of Islam, would hold sway.

Two aspects of this demand for a 'Muslim' state need to be noted. First, this was to be a 'Muslim-majority' state. The Muslim-majority provinces of north-western and north-eastern India would be constituted into separate blocks, with minor adjustments if necessary in existing provincial boundaries. The plan entailed a minimal disturbance in the demographic distribution of Hindus and Muslims, the communities they lived in, and local social and economic arrangements.

'The Pakistan movement, as envisaged by Mr Jinnah, [does not] require any uprooting of associations and ties of homeland which have existed for generations by an interchange of populations from the Hindu majority provinces to the Muslim majority provinces,' declared Hassan Suhrawardy in November 1942.[11] Or, as a Muslim student of Lucknow University in 1946-47 recalled, 'nobody thought in terms of migration in those days: [the Muslims] all thought that everything would remain the same, Punjab would remain Punjab, Sindh would remain Sindh, there won't be any demographic changes – no drastic changes anyway – the Hindus and Sikhs would continue to live in Pakistan... and we would continue to live in India.'[12]

'Pakistan' was to be a Muslim-dominated state, to balance a Hindu-dominated 'Hindustan'. This is why Jinnah and the Muslim League were ready to accept the Cabinet Mission Plan. In the words of a leading supporter of Jinnah, 'The Muslim League accepted the Cabinet Mission's Plan, as it met the *substance of the demand for Pakistan* and kept the way open for the emergence of a sovereign Pakistan in case the union centre functioned to the detriment of the Muslim provinces.'[13] A group of Punjabi Muslims put the point even more strongly on the Muslim League's withdrawal of its earlier acceptance of the Mission's scheme. 'The most important part of the Scheme is complete provincial autonomy,' they noted, '... this is, for all practical purposes, *real Pakistan*. One wonders what more the Pakistan of our Leaders' conception can give us.'[14]

In spite of all the militancy of propaganda and demands on

different sides in the last months and years of British rule, the idea of 'Pakistan' remained remarkably vague. It was never clarified how Muslims spread out over the subcontinent, and divided by class, sect, gender, regional interests and language, would become part of *one* separate country; or indeed exactly where this new state called 'Pakistan' would be. In any event, there was little desire to move from long-established 'homes' – the *vatan* or *desh*, homeland, country and native place. Indeed, for numerous supporters of Pakistan, for much of the period up to August 1947, the object was to gain assured Muslim dominance in the Muslim-majority zones of north-western and north-eastern India, without any substantial change in existing provincial boundaries or any significant movement of populations.

Many in Punjab and Bengal, even among supporters of the League and the Pakistan movement in the mid-1940s, had reservations about the theory that the Hindus and Muslims of the entire subcontinent formed two separate and homogenous nations. Abul Hashim, Secretary of the Bengal Muslim League, declared: 'Liberated India must necessarily be, as God has made it, a subcontinent having complete independence for every nation inhabiting it...' While this could be seen, at a stretch, as a statement in favour of the two-nation theory, it reads more obviously as the advocacy of not two, but several nations: 'a subcontinent' with 'complete independence for every nation inhabiting it' – Bengal, Punjab, Sindh, and so on.[15]

When Hindu, Sikh and Congress leaders proposed the partition of Bengal and Punjab, neither Jinnah nor the Punjab and Bengal Leaguers were pleased. In April 1947, Jinnah pleaded with Mountbatten not to play with the unity of Bengal and Punjab which have 'national characteristics in common: common history, common ways of life', and where 'the Hindus have stronger feelings as Bengalis or Punjabis than they have as members of the Congress'. Liaqat Ali Khan, the first prime minister of Pakistan, echoed the sentiment. The Bengal Muslim League leader, Husain Suhrawardy, asked the Viceroy to postpone a decision on Partition until November 1947 to give his 'united Bengal' scheme a little more time to succeed. Fazlul Haq, mover of the original 'Pakistan' resolution in Lahore in 1940, expressed the opinion even more strongly, declaring that the British should stay on, rather than partition the country.[16]

Nevertheless, for a whole variety of reasons that historians have investigated at length,[17] the campaign for an independent nation-state for the Muslims of the subcontinent gathered unprecedented momentum in the years 1946 and 1947, and the outbreak of massive violence between groups of Hindus, Muslims and Sikhs in different parts of the subcontinent lent it great urgency. Partition followed. What this has meant for the very substantial Muslim population that remained in India has not always been fully appreciated. The 'Muslim problem' in India now became the problem of a 'suspect' population, of so-called 'closet-Pakistanis', people who had already shown their disloyalty to the 'nation' – in the movement for the establishment of an independent Pakistan – and who could easily turn against its interests at any time.

The process of Partition had claimed large numbers of lives, and destroyed the peace and well-being of innumerable individuals and families, even before official Partition and Independence occurred on 15 August 1947. Within weeks after that date, it would destroy many more, and uproot practically a whole countryside in Punjab and neighbouring areas, as people fled in both directions in search of minimal safety and security. In Bengal, the movement of 'minorities' did not assume quite the same proportions as in the north-west. The migrations were far from being insubstantial, but they occurred on a smaller scale than in Punjab, and were more spread out in time, coming in waves that were observable in East Bengal in 1948, the 1950s and even later. For all that, the minorities lived in fear all over the partitioned subcontinent in 1947-48. There was simply too much evidence of families and fortunes destroyed on account of nothing but their religious affiliation; and far too many reports and rumours of rape, abduction and forced religious conversion – from near and far.

Towards the end of September 1947, Nehru, then prime minister of India, remarked that only those Hindus or Muslims should stay in the country who considered it their own nation, gave it their undivided loyalty, and refused to look to any outside agency for help. Removed from the confusion, suspicions and violence of the time, this was an unexceptionable statement. But as the Calcutta daily, *The Statesman*, commented in its editorial of 5 October 1947, 'how were the Muslims of India to prove their loyalty when the very act of fleeing in fear from their homes was interpreted as a sign of disloyalty and extra-territorial attachment?'

In November 1947, it was reported that nearly 5000 Muslim railwaymen who had earlier opted for service in Pakistan, had now 'set the authorities a serious problem' by withdrawing their preference for Pakistan and refusing to leave India. With this change of heart, they unfortunately laid themselves open to the charge of being Pakistani agents, engaged in a conspiracy, although their motives were almost certainly more mundane, the result of news of troubles on that side of the border too, and of the fact that migrating to and settling in Pakistan was never going to be easy or smooth. However, even their co-workers in Uttar Pradesh were not inclined to be generous in their response to this change. Hindu railwaymen in Lucknow threatened to go on strike if the 'Pakistan personnel' were allowed to stay, and the railway authorities insisted that those who had opted for service in Pakistan must now go.[18]

A letter from one such railway worker, and the Indian

government's response to it, provides another illustration of the hopelessness of many choices. The letter was written in September 1947 by Safdar Ali Khan, 'Guard, Moradabad', to the Secretary, 'Partition Department', Government of India. Headed 'Permission to revise my decision "to serve in India"', it said:

I had submitted my final choice to serve in Pakistan. ... The persuasions of my fellow-workers and friends favoured [forced?] me to come to this decision at which I am rubbing my hands now [sic]. ... My old mother is lying very seriously ill and she is not in a mood to allow me to go to Pakistan as she has no hope to survive her illness. ... I have blundered in favour of Pakistan. Really speaking, as I have stated above, the decision was not my own but ... made under compulsion. I am an Indian first and an Indian last. I want to live in India and die in India ... Hence I humbly request your honour to permit me to revise my decision and allow me to serve in India.'[19]

Maulana Abul Kalam Azad, the Education Minister of India, forwarded this letter to the Home Minister, Vallabhbhai Patel, who responded briefly: 'The Partition Council decision has been that once a final choice is made it should be adhered to. I [can] see no prospect, therefore, of the gentleman, whose application you have sent me, being allowed to change his option now.'[20]

There is a bureaucratic imperative at work here. Two new state administrations are being set up, rules have to be made and followed. But there is a moral imperative as well. People simply have to decide where they stand and who they are, once and for all. This was a demand that was made insistently of the Muslim minority in the new India. The modern state insists on a separation between the public and the private. Yet Partition produced a situation in which the private (the 'Hindu' in India, and the 'Muslim' in Pakistan) articulated itself as the public, while denying that possibility to the other. The developments of the

1980s and '90s in India that I referred to in the previous section
have only served to further accentuate the problem.

hindu assertiveness

It may help to step back at this point and rehearse the matter of
the freezing of religious and other assemblages into recognised
communities (or 'minorities') in colonial and post-colonial India
since this was obviously not a process that began with the coming
of independence and the nation-state. It was in the nineteenth
century that propagandists and publicists among the Hindu,
Muslim, Sikh and other religious groupings in India moved to
appropriate marginal populations (the 'Untouchables' came to be
classified as unambiguously Hindu for the first time by Hindu
leaders), to purify their communities ('Muslims' must not be
contaminated by 'Hindu' practices, and vice versa), and to
establish distinct and separate identities (among religious
groupings, most notably in the case of the Sikhs). In this way,
notions of an 'all-India Hindu community', an 'all-India Muslim
community' and a new 'Sikh community' distinct from the
Hindus gradually took hold in the later nineteenth and early
twentieth centuries.

Partition significantly hastened these processes, and for
some time in 1947-48, it was as if great numbers of people all
over northern India were marked by nothing but their Muslim-
ness, Hindu-ness, or Sikh-ness. Communities like the large
peasant caste of Mevs in the Mewati region south and west of
Delhi, which had worn their Islam lightly for centuries and were
described by observers (and sometimes by themselves) as 'half-
Hindu and half-Muslim,' came to be treated now as Muslims
plain and simple who in the view of many were best dispatched to
Pakistan.[21]

Even after the experience of Partition, however, the
identification of 'Muslim' and 'foreigner' was not so readily made

in many parts of the country. The anthropologist David Pocock's account of a Gujarat village illustrates the point very well indeed. There were four poor Muslim households in the village Pocock studied in the mid-1950s. Two of them were called Vora, the other two Sipai, the former derived from the Shiah sect of Bohras, and the latter indicating that some ancestor had been a soldier. One or two pictures in their houses suggested Shiah allegiance, but (says Pocock) these Muslims knew nothing of Shiah-Sunni or other sectarian differences. 'Similarly the Prophet was represented as a holy man, one of many, who was born in India and was the originator of the sect to which they belong.' The children were given Muslim names and sons were circumcised, but the families followed customary Hindu rules of property and succession, participated in Hindu ceremonies in the village, and were treated much as a Hindu caste by the other villagers.[22]

Throughout western India, Bohras and Khojas were recognised as Muslim groups of a special kind: practical businessmen, speakers of Gujarati, well integrated into the local society and culture – more like the Parsis of Bombay than the 'turbulent' Muslims of north and north-western India (and Pakistan).[23] However, sustained campaigns of anti-Muslim propaganda and the major conflicts of the last few decades have nullified the benefits of such exceptionalism as well. In March and April, 2002, even the rural Muslims of Gujarat, Bohras and Khojas among them, were not spared by the Hindu assailants who spread terror and death among Muslims throughout the state.

Thus the forging of new kinds of Muslim, Sikh and Hindu identity provided the basis for new kinds of struggles for Muslim and Sikh homelands in the middle and later twentieth century (to be matched, in the last couple of decades, by the most ironic of them all – the movement for a 'Hindu' homeland in the Hindu-majority country of India). Since the 1980s, as I have noted, arguments have been advanced about how the Hindu majority must unite to avoid being overwhelmed by the minority, how the minority (tied to international forces of various kinds) must not be allowed to hold the nation to ransom, and how it must most certainly no longer be appeased.

In India, as already mentioned, part of the context for this was provided by the collapse of earlier constituencies (most notably, perhaps, the alliance between the highest castes and the lowest, along with the Muslims, who had brought the Congress back to power in the 1950s and '60s), and by a new politics of coalitions, 'pragmatism' (or *real-politik* as it is sometimes called) and a 'make your fortune while you can' mentality. In this situation, Hindu right-wing forces (but not these forces alone, since the entire political spectrum has shifted to the right, in India as in other parts of the world) were able to generate a heightened rhetoric of 'natural' national unity, based now not on a political vision and programme for the future, but on religious symbols described as the nation's fundamental heritage. The new commercialisation and the much more evident flattening of cultures that came with neo-liberalism contributed to this phenomenon. An increasingly influential group of non-resident Indians, seeking identity and self-definition, now became ardent, long-distance nationalists – fervent supporters of the battle for new Sikh and Muslim homelands and the destruction of a disused (but beautiful) sixteenth century mosque in Ayodhya – not on the basis of any historical debate or political struggle, but rather of the most excessively invested, and reductionist, symbols of nation, community and religion.[24]

With such support, and with the backing of well-entrenched and well-trained police and para-military forces, right-wing parties in some regions of India have more or less successfully re-invented the nation-state in a chauvinist Hindu image and successfully cowed down the minorities. Muslims in India, and increasingly the very small community of Christians too, have come under suspicion because of their link to 'foreign' (anti-national) religions, hence 'foreign' (anti-national) forces, and more recently in the case of the Muslims to what is widely proclaimed as a worldwide network of terrorism.

Since the terrorist attacks on New York and Washington on 11 September 2001, the 'war against terror' has become an instrument in the hands of numerous powerful groups and states in different parts of the world, India, Pakistan, Russia and Israel among them, to settle old scores and make easy (financial and political) gains. There was large-scale international public opposition at one point to the war against Iraq. However, opposition to the longer term strategies adopted by governments far and wide in their efforts to combat 'terror' has been muted at best; and there has been little by way of a challenge to the nationalist, and even 'humanitarian', arguments advanced in justification of their actions. Governments and bureaucracies have in any case over time accumulated extensive powers to do as they want, largely unchallenged – because of their invisibility, their access to information, and an easy recourse to arguments about the sanctity of national interests, above all, the interest of national security. Over the last few years, this exercise of bureaucratic, state power has become increasingly arbitrary and unquestioned.

Today this is a notable condition of politics in the world's largest democracies, as they are commonly proclaimed, both India and the USA. Opposition to these developments, especially from the organised mainstream political parties, has been restricted to condemnations of government for its poor timing or its failure to pursue 'nationalist' policies (such as anti-terrorist measures, militarisation, or nuclearisation!) vigorously enough. Large sections of the population have lived in a kind of 'security state' even in these leading democracies, with increasing restrictions on what official policies may be debated, let alone combated.

In many parts of the world, I submit, the area of religious belief and observance, and more generally that of cultural practice, is very much subject to this new, illiberal regime. These must now, perhaps more than ever before, conform to the definitions (and prescriptions) of the 'mainstream'. Instead of a constitutionally guaranteed right to diversity of faith and worship and a struggle for tolerance and understanding based upon that, what we have had in India recently is an *intolerance* not so much of particular religious practices or beliefs, as of the simple fact of existence of people belonging to other religious denominations. Two slogans that were widely touted in Ayodhya (in 1990 and 1992) and Gujarat (in 2002) sum up the new politics of violence that comes with this intolerance. The first, '*Musalman ke do hi sthaan, Pakistan ya kabristan*', left no space at all for the existence of Muslims in the nation-state of India. The second, '*Pahle Qasai, phir Isai*', extended the argument to the small Christian community of the country as well.

Fortunately, the clock appears to have been turned back a little with the results of the last election, and the coming to power of a Congress-led coalition which is rather more concerned about the protection of the minorities than the Bharatiya Janata Party-led coalition it replaced. In this new phase of Indian politics, the forces of Hindutva, or a narrow right-wing Hindu nationalism, have come up against the mobilisation of regional causes and, more broadly, of lower castes and classes seeking to link up with deprived minorities (such as the Muslims) in an alliance that they call the *bahujan samaj* – literally, the 'majority society'. It is time to turn to this lower caste politics now.

the dalit struggle

The politics of lower caste assertion points to another fault line of nationhood and democracy in India, the divide between a respectable, upper-caste, culturally and economically privileged elite and the mass of poor, illiterate and 'polluting' people who have for too long been kept at the bottom of society. A critical aspect of the struggle for democratic rights in the Indian nation-state relates obviously to the situation of the latter. One gets a reasonably good sense of the issues involved through an examination of the history and politics of an increasingly visible lower caste and lower class category – a group of people who were (and still are) parcelled out into innumerable smaller castes, altogether called Untouchables, Harijans, Scheduled Castes or Dalits.[25]

The history of caste in India has followed a surprising course – from a freezing of the country into a 'caste' society by colonial sociology, to a nationalist belief that caste was a relic of the past that would disappear with the development of modernity and democracy, to lower caste attempts to upgrade their status by appropriating the beliefs and practices of the upper castes (what M.N. Srinivas called 'Sanskritisation'), to the current stage of lower caste assertion of a lower caste status in order to demand state support and recompense. From the 1970s onwards, the Dalit political and ideological struggle has been led by a new Dalit intellectual, professional and administrative elite, itself the product of reservations in educational and administrative institutions. And the most striking feature of their political agenda has been the belief that social change and advance will come not through piecemeal reform, or even reservations, but through the capture of political power.

Truthful relations between Hindus and Muslims, bread for the masses, and the abolition of untouchability: these were the conditions of *swaraj* or self-rule as advocated by Gandhi in the mid-1920s. 'Bread for the masses' is not a slogan that is heard very much in India or indeed much of the rest of the world today, which has more to do with the demand for free markets and unfettered opportunities for profit than with the availability of food in particularly great abundance.[26] The question of relations between Hindus and Muslims was supposed to be resolved through Partition. This was a resolution that was perhaps doomed from the start: and we have noted some of its consequences. Finally, Untouchability was abolished by a clause in the Indian Constitution of 1950: and various rounds of legislation since the 1950s have sought to give teeth to this constitutional revolution. Not surprisingly, the results have been somewhat mixed here as well.

Dalit spokespersons have sometimes argued that the establishment of British rule, with its notion of law, or at least of a criminal law that would apply equally to all the people,[27] constitutes for them a first moment of liberation, the first opportunity they had obtained in a long period of history to fight for anything like equal rights and a dignified place in society. Others among them have noted that the period of mass democracy from 1950 onwards has, for all its imperfections, been the 'brightest' period in Dalit history, enabling Dalit groups to organise themselves, obtain education and access to public office and even some political power, and thereby to overcome some of the worst forms of oppression and disability.[28] The task for Dalit leaders has been to find the most advantageous arrangements for the pursuit of this struggle for social justice and political equality. An important part of their endeavour has been the attempt to gain political recognition and rights as a minority.

What makes the Dalit claim to minority status particularly interesting is the historical location of Dalit groups and individuals on the boundaries of Hindu society – not apart from it, but not quite part of it either. As movements for modern definitions of religion and religious community developed in the later nineteenth and early twentieth centuries, and the question of numbers gained importance, Hindu leaders and reformers became active in the effort to 'reclaim' the Dalits and 're-educate' them in their identity as Hindus. Yet, given the character of Hindu society, the organisation of different classes and vocational groups into distinct castes, and the overriding concern with issues of purity and pollution, all the indications were that the Dalits would have to remain very *lowly* Hindus – a 'minority' that could not be made part of the 'majority', but that the majority would not treat as a minority either.

The Dalits themselves had an ambivalent, fragmentary, relationship with this majority. The politics of colonial and post-colonial India gave them a new opportunity to challenge the inherited structures and relations of power amid which they lived. As the religious communities of the subcontinent went about 'purifying' and reconstituting themselves, and as urbanization and migration, educational opportunities and political consciousness grew, numerous Dalits responded with questions about existing social and political arrangements, and demanded greater access to the resources of the modern society and state. One part of this effort was the attempt by Dalit leaders to redefine the Dalits as a historically distinct community, and to seek safeguards for it (such as separate electorates and the reservation of seats in legislative bodies and public services) of the kind that had been granted to other minority communities in the early twentieth century.

It was on the matter of separate representation for the Dalits that B. R. Ambedkar, perhaps the outstanding Dalit leader of the twentieth century, and Mohandas Gandhi, the predominant leader of the Indian National Congress, disagreed most sharply. The differences between them reached a climax in 1932, when the British government announced a communal award that included the grant of separate electorates to Untouchables in the areas of their greatest concentration. This award followed negotiations that had stalled – among other things on the issue of separate electorates for Untouchables – at the Round Table Conferences held in London to work out the details of a revised framework for the continued government of India under British control.

Gandhi, and others in the Congress, saw the grant of separate electorates – and the earlier demand for it by Dalit leaders – as a way of splitting and therefore weakening the Hindu community, a development that would only compound what the British had already accomplished through their institution of separate electorates for Muslims. Ambedkar, by contrast, saw separate electorates as an essential lever in the struggle to advance the downtrodden castes. He was forced to give in in 1932, unable to resist the pressure brought to bear upon him by the fast-unto-death that Gandhi launched against this extension of separate electorates. However the way in which the conflict played out left him deeply embittered, and he seems never to have forgiven Gandhi and the Congress for what he saw as their betrayal.[29]

The issues involved in the clash between Ambedkar and Gandhi were brought into even sharper focus with the acquisition of citizenship by all the inhabitants of the country, the institution of universal adult franchise, and the abolition of untouchability in the constitution of independent India, adopted in 1950. At one level, what was at stake in the Dalit struggle before and after Independence was the question of differential access to the state and its resources. What was equally at issue, however, was a question of pride and human dignity, the question precisely of being equal citizens in a modern, democratic society. That struggle has shown no signs of abating; on the contrary, it has grown in strength at both of these levels.

Some of the most urgent political debates of the 1940s and '50s related, I have suggested, to the question of the rights of minorities, and indeed to the question: who are the minorities? The Dalits laid claim to being a minority, even a 'nation', like the

Muslims and the Sikhs. Several Dalit spokespersons even advanced an argument for a separate *Achutistan*, to match the Muslims' 'Pakistan'. A special Scheduled Castes Political Conference held at Allahabad in December 1942 declared that 'India [was] not a nation but ... a constellation of nations,' one of which was the nation of Untouchables or Scheduled Castes.[30] Ambedkar apparently made the same sort of claim in 1944. He is reported to have said that Gandhi and Jinnah were making a serious mistake in holding exclusive talks on the constitutional future of India, for '[b]esides the Hindus and Muslims, the Scheduled Castes are a third necessary party'. And again, a few days later, that the Scheduled Castes were 'no part of the Hindu community, but constituted a different nation'.[31]

At other times, he was more circumspect, arguing at length that the Dalits were 'a separate element in the national life of India,' that the refusal to allow this minority its proper representation was precisely the political problem of the Untouchables, that the attention Congress paid to the place of the Muslims should not be at the expense of 'the other communities who need more protection,' and that the executive power in the government of independent India should have its 'mandate not only from the majority [Hindus] but also from the minorities [Muslims, Sikhs, Christians, Dalits and so on] in the Legislature.'[32] With this last argument, put forward in a 1945 speech on the 'Communal Deadlock and a Way to Solve It', Ambedkar also suggested 'a rule of unanimity' as the principle of decision making in the legislature and the executive. This would put an end to the communal problem, he declared.[33]

In making this proposal, the Dalit leader overlooked the internally differentiated and contested character of community as well as national politics in the subcontinent. In the event, the 'minorities' failed to gain anything like a veto power in the political processes of the new India. In the exultation of the moment, and the aftermath of Partition, no communal grouping was to be permitted to challenge the unity of the nation again, and anyone who urged political differentiation among India's citizens on grounds of religious or caste community was put on the defensive. Religious groups (majority and minority) were guaranteed the protection of their religious institutions and the freedom to profess and practise their faiths. However, the independent state would have no differential 'political' rights for religious or social minorities, except for a ten-year period of grace during which limited support – in the form of reservations in legislatures and government services – was to be provided to the most depressed castes and sub-castes.[34]

For the Dalits, there was an additional difficulty. While Ambedkar and others sought to obtain recognition of Untouchables as a minority, no different from Muslims, Sikhs, Christians, Anglo-Indians and other such minorities, the fact is that the Untouchables, Outcastes, Depressed Classes, Harijans, Scheduled Castes, whatever the name we might use for them, gained their distinctiveness – at least until they were constituted into a legally recognised minority – precisely from the fact of their untouchability, that is, the discrimination they suffered at the hands of Hindu society. Gandhi was, as always, quick to point out the contradiction in this position. 'We do not want on our register and on our census Untouchables classified as a separate class,' he declared at the Round Table Conference in London in 1931. 'Sikhs may remain as such in perpetuity, so may Muhammadans, so may Europeans. Will Untouchables remain Untouchables in perpetuity?'[35]

In this respect, the Dalits were caught in an extraordinary bind – that of being Hindus and non-Hindus at one and the same time. Consider the ambivalence that appears in Ambedkar's presentation, as law minister, of the case for the reform of the personal law of the Hindus. At one stage in the debate on the Hindu Code Bill, he referred to the Hindu *shastras* as 'your *shastras*'. To a member's interjection ('Your *shastras*?'), he responded by saying, 'Yes, because I belong to the other caste,' and, a little later, 'I am an unusual member of the Hindu community.'[36] At another point in the same debate, he spoke of 'our ancient ideals, which are to my judgement, most archaic and impossible for anybody to practice.'[37] There was clearly no easy escape from the aggrandizing character of 'Hinduism' even for a leader who had declared, fifteen years earlier: 'I had the misfortune of being born with the stigma of [being] an Untouchable.... It is not my fault; but I will not die a Hindu, for this is in my power.'[38]

Paradoxically, then, it was precisely their untouchability that Dalit leaders had to assert in order to try and gain recognition as a 'minority', with the safeguards and rights appropriate to a minority in a democratic republic. More, once the principle of affirmative action and reservations had been accepted, to give the disadvantaged and 'backward' classes a fairer chance in the life of the republic, this 'minority' status as an Untouchable community was what Ambedkar and others had to fight to preserve even after the formal conversion of particular Dalit groups to Buddhism, Christianity or other religions. Witness Ambedkar's comment in the course of his speech on the occasion of the mass conversion to Buddhism that he led on 15 October 1956 – 'Even after conversion to Buddhism, I am confident, I [or 'we', the Dalit community] will get the political rights'[39] – and the demands made in recent years by groups of Christian and Muslim Dalits for an extension of the benefits of reservations to them.

An important part of the Dalit political argument, from the days of B. R. Ambedkar and E. V. Ramaswami Naicker (or 'Periyar', the great leader, another colossus of lower caste politics in the first half of the twentieth century), has come in the form of a statement about numbers and the need for proportionate political representation. The militant Dalit movement of the last twenty years has underlined both the numerical strength of the oppressed and the need for affirmative action to right historical wrongs. Witness the slogans:

> *Mat hamara, raj tumhara*
> *Nahin chalega, nahin chalega*
> (Our votes, and your rule
> This will be allowed no longer).

Or again,

> *Vote se lenge PM/CM*
> *Aarakshan se SP/DM*
>> (We shall obtain the positions of prime minister
>> and chief minister through our votes;
>> And the rank of superintendent of police and
>> district magistrate through reservations.)[40]

Recent ideologues and leaders have also returned to the late nineteenth century thinker, Jyotirao Phule's notion of the *bahujan samaj* (the majority of the people), long and unnecessarily oppressed by a small elite (the *shetji-bhatji samaj* of traders and priests, the unscrupulous moneyed and educated classes). Thus Kanshi Ram, founder of BAMCEF (the All-India Backward and Minority Communities' Employees Federation) and subsequently of the Bahujan Samaj Party, declared: 'The *bahujan samaj* accounts for 85 per cent of the votes. It is a shame that the foreign Aryans constituting 15 per cent are ruling over the 85 per cent... An Aryan ruler can never work for our betterment... When our ancestors from the *bahujan samaj* were ruling over the country, India was known all over the world for its prosperity...'[41]

The link between the *bahujan samaj* and the original inhabitants of the country, who were conquered and ruled by a colonising body of Aryan invaders, remains an important part of Dalit discourse, although it has now been extensively questioned by historians. But the more powerful claim is that of being 85 per cent of the people, and the right of a majority as great as this to rule in a democracy. What Ambedkar and his followers attempted to bring about through mass agitation, constitutional protection and conversion, the standard bearers of Dalit politics today have sought to accomplish through electoral struggle and strategic alliances.

The current turbulence in Indian society and state, the collapse of an earlier, stable political and administrative arrangement, the gradual erosion of traditional caste and class power, and the growing self-confidence and strength of hitherto suppressed castes and classes, has helped the lower castes and classes, often in alliance with the major religious minorities, in their attempt to change the balance of power. To quote Kanshi Ram again, 'Stability does not help us. We are looking for an unstable polity. That helps us consolidate our position.'[42]

What stands out in the recent course of the Dalit movement is the attempted mobilisation of a Dalit electoral constituency on a provincial and then a countrywide scale, and a politics of alliance with any party that might help in the Dalit accumulation of power – something that many political observers have derided as unprincipled and corrupt. Whatever one's view on that – and let us not forget that corruption and lack of principles are not features of lower caste politics alone – the results have been significant.

internal colonialism?

It will help to conclude these reflections on the fault lines of Indian nationhood with a few comments on the question of 'internal colonialism', a charge that has been laid, directly or indirectly, by a number of Dalit spokespersons as well as by Muslims and others in the India since the 1940s.

In the Dalit and Muslim instances, we are dealing of course with populations that are widely distributed in a 'national' territory, and that have come in time to some kind of mutual accommodation with more privileged, numerous and powerful groups, although they have done so in a markedly hierarchical manner. The political question in such examples is this: what happens to the 'minority', to Muslims or Dalits in India (or to African-Americans in the USA), if the 'majority' gains an apparently unfettered right to rule and to lord it over the 'minorities', and a sense of colonialism persists even after the establishment of formal democracy? It is in this context that we might understand Ambedkar's comment on a new, and in his view unjust, tax levied by the Congress government on the lowly Mahar population of Bombay Presidency in 1939: 'It is good that the Congress has revealed itself so soon and that it did not wait till it had secured full *swaraj* when it would have been so terribly difficult to remedy matters.' [43]

Owing to a number of developments after 1946, the situation has changed in a number of respects. Ambedkar became India's first law minister and the helmsman in the framing of the nation's constitution. Even so, some might argue that the concessions to Dalit leaders were still largely symbolic in the early decades of Indian independence (at least at the national level). However that might be, the agitations and elections of recent years have radically transformed the situation. The Bahujan Samaj Party has emerged as a major player in the politics of several north Indian states and at the centre, and Mayawati, leader of the party in Uttar Pradesh, has not only gained the honour of becoming India's first Dalit woman chief minister but has also been returned to power more than once. Statues of B. R. Ambedkar have appeared in the central lobby of Parliament as well as in thousands of village squares and urban crossroads across the country, making him perhaps the most memorialised Indian political leader of all. A Dalit civil servant, K. R. Narayanan, who retired after a very successful career in the elite Indian Foreign Service, was elected vice-president and then president of India, serving with distinction in both positions. The kaleidoscope of the nation has shifted just a little.

Progress – if that is the word – has not been quite so clear-cut in the case of India's Muslims, as we have seen. Yet, the holding of periodic elections where the electorate has been allowed some choice, ongoing debates about the national interest and the just society, and the very fact of living in a new India that is confusing and confounding, oppressive and demanding, disorganised and argumentative (warts and all) has allowed a significant level of political participation and led the majority of political spokespersons and tendencies among Muslims as well as Dalits to dispense with the category of internal colonialism in their political expressions. Among political leaders and movements speaking for a number of regional nationalities on the northern and north-eastern borders of the Indian state, however, the charge of a continuing colonialism, or internal colonialism, has not lost force quite so perceptibly .

In three areas – Kashmir, Punjab and the states and territories of the Northeast – all of which border on neighbouring countries (China and Pakistan) where disgruntled forces have in the past found refuge and sustenance, the Indian nation-state has had to confront a variety of breakaway movements. The particular conjuncture of historical circumstances, needs and grievances that gave rise to separatist movements, insurgencies and conflicts in these areas varies enormously, and it would take us too far afield to undertake a detailed discussion of all of these. What I will do instead is to focus on a few, limited aspects of New Delhi's relations with the Northeast, which will perhaps suffice to indicate the consequences of inadequately democratic forms of governance, and of government that appears to the governed as rule from afar.

The political boundaries of the Northeast (the point applies to the frontiers of other parts of India, as it does to the boundaries of other nation-states) were of course arbitrarily constructed. In this instance, the boundaries were determined to a large extent by the accident of the limits and arrangements of British colonial rule: 'colonial geography as destiny,' as one scholar describes it.[44] As it happened, the frontier between British India and China was never entirely clarified, leaving uncertain grey zones, disputed territories and discontented peoples demanding various degrees of autonomy, or independence, on both sides of the border. The boundaries between India and Burma (Myanmar), which was separated from British India in 1935, and between India and Bangladesh (part of the wider cultural and administrative entity of Bengal, until its partition into West Bengal and East Pakistan in 1947) are equally arbitrary. Modern state power, however, has its consequences, and it is within (or against) these stipulated boundaries that the people of the area have had to seek out political futures.

From the 1930s and to some extent earlier, voices in the colonial government had made an argument about the need to separate the 'backward', hill or tribal tracts from the remainder of the north-eastern British Indian province of Assam. 'If the tribal areas fell under the control of elected Indian legislatures they would be ruined,' one said. The Nagas in particular 'must not be converted from good Nagas or whatever they are [sic.] into bad Hindus,' said another.[45] One result of this kind of thinking had been the establishment of various territories that were 'excluded' from the main lines of Indian political development (and, one might add, economic and cultural development as well). These are exclusions that have continued to bedevil the post-colonial Indian regime too.

There were rumours in 1946 that the departing colonial government planned to carve out a new state, strategically located on the borders of India, East Pakistan, Burma, China and Tibet, by amalgamating the hill areas of Burma with parts of the hill areas of Assam and what is now Arunachal Pradesh.[46] While this came to nought, the governor of Assam, Sir Akbar Hydari, signed an accord with the Naga National Council, which gave the right to the people of the Naga Hills 'to develop themselves according to their freely expressed wishes' in all judicial, fiscal and cultural matters. The agreement added that after ten years the Naga National Council would be asked whether they wished to extend the accord or renegotiate it. Not entirely unexpectedly, the government of independent India refused to take any notice of this agreement.[47] Insurgency and counter-insurgency operations have followed in the succeeding years, disrupting daily routines and taking a large toll on life and property.

To understand something of the Indian nationalist response to insurgency and independence movements in the Northeast, it is necessary to remind ourselves of the extraordinary stake that all nations appear to have in the preservation of their 'territorial integrity'. What Sankaran Krishna calls a 'cartographic anxiety'[48] has preyed on the minds of the rulers and spokespersons of the Indian nation-state from the moment of its birth. One might extend the argument further. Once the map of 'Mother India' had been imagined in the later nineteenth and early twentieth centuries along the lines of colonial India (however uncertain and recent the boundaries of the latter might have been), there was little room for concession in the minds of the nationalists. The experience of Partition only led to a hardening of the commitment to national unity and territorial integrity.

Over time, the political map of the Northeast has changed completely, but the concern to retain New Delhi's control as a measure of national unity has remained undiluted. One response to the Naga insurgency, and the demands for Naga self-rule, was the separation of the Naga areas from Assam and the establishment in 1963 of the state of Nagaland. However, it is indicative of the short-sightedness of India's rulers, and the bureaucratic mentality that goes into the administration of much of the Northeast, that the apex body overseeing the affairs of Nagaland until the 1970s was the External Affairs rather than the Home Ministry. In 1966, rebellion broke out among the Mizos living in the Mizo Hills district of Assam. To deal with this, the district was converted into a Union Territory in 1972 and into a full-fledged state subsequently.

The wholesale re-organisation of the Northeast occurred after the military debacle in the border war with China in 1962 and the military intervention that helped to establish the independent country of Bangladesh in 1971. It was after 1962 that the Indian government turned earnestly to the 'development' of the remoter areas, with the building of roads and bridges, rest houses, airports and other means of communication. The Northeast Frontier Agency, created in 1954 out of the North East Frontier Tracts (one of the 'excluded areas' of colonial Assam), was given its own legislature in 1969, made into a Union Territory in 1972 and established as a separate state, Arunachal Pradesh, in 1987. Seven different states (Assam, Arunachal Pradesh, Meghalaya, Nagaland, Tripura, Manipur and Mizoram) now populate what is called the Northeast. Elections are held regularly, and 'development' funds continue to be allocated to the region. Yet the sense of alienation of many of its people has not significantly declined.

Closer to Hanoi than to New Delhi as the crow flies, India's Northeast remains poorly linked with the rest of the country and even more poorly understood. Bureaucrats from other provinces asked to serve in the region often talk of a two- or three-year 'exile', of 'border postings' and even 'punishment posts'. This is symptomatic of the view of the Northeast held by the majority of functionaries of the Indian state. Equally indicative of its isolation, and its untypical place in the history of a democratic nation-state, is the continuous, and heavy, presence of the Indian military; the special permits required (even by Indian nationals not native to the region) to visit most parts of it; and the role of the Indian army as the major entrepreneur over much of the territory (in Arunachal Pradesh, Nagaland and Mizoram and beyond), chief investor and builder of roads and bridges, and the leading arm of 'development'. Not surprisingly, in this context, Mizos and Nagas and Bodos and other local communities speak in their turn of visitors 'from India', or of themselves 'visiting India' and of being treated like foreigners there (in view of their Mongoloid features). In one famous incident, a chief minister of Nagaland is said to have been asked to produce his passport when he was checking into a five-star hotel in Bombay.[49]

The process of 'development', even in its more recent phases in which sections of the local population have been active partners, adds to the general sense of alienation. Some of the new capital cities of the region have become ugly urban sprawls, dominated by corruption and concrete. The increasing numbers of governmental and quasi-governmental agencies and offices have brought with them an explosion in the number of cars and other motor vehicles. All this, and the growing migration of local populations into these new towns where employment opportunities are largely concentrated, has led to great congestion, pedestrian-unfriendly roads, repeated traffic jams and intense air pollution – the exact opposite of what one would expect in these lush, heavily forested and, until recently, unspoilt hills.

Among the chief beneficiaries of the increase in development funds for the Northeast are numerous contractors and licence holders from other parts of India, short-term 'immigrants' out to make money in any way they can. One civil servant with long experience of service in the region has argued that as such resources have grown in response to expressions of discontent by local groups and political parties, there has in fact been a 'quicker siphoning off of funds to the heartland', alongside the accrual of benefits to those in power locally 'through the usual corrupt forces of the licence-permit raj'. What this has produced is a succession of increasingly corrupt regimes in one state after another, throughout the region.[50] It is scarcely surprising, as the political analyst Sanjib Baruah puts it, that 'insurgent groups in Assam and the northeast have sometimes successfully isolated state governments that are seen as being in league with these [outside] adventurer-entrepreneurs, and have targeted some people who are perceived as heartland adventurer-entrepreneurs as the "enemy"'.[51] What makes matters worse is that insurgent factions have begun to compete with these 'adventurer-entrepreneurs' for a share in the loot. The spirals of colonialism and internal colonialism extend a long way.

conclusion

One last word on the issue of nationhood. If, as I have suggested, twentieth century nationalisms were aimed first and foremost at the overthrow of imperialism and autocracy, then democracy was clearly a most potent, perhaps a fundamental plank. What the history of the north-eastern states of India, and of Punjab and Kashmir, suggests is that full political participation is no less important than the question of cultural belonging in the career of the nation-state. The engaged political participation of a functioning democracy rests as much on the question of dignity, a sense of justice and fair-play, and a respect for cultural, social and political difference, as it does on the institution of adult franchise and the holding of periodic elections.

What is crucial is the willingness to negotiate, and re-negotiate, political settlements between social, cultural and political tendencies and associations that are varied and changing, in New Delhi, the Northeast, and in other Indian states. This is what nationalism has not always been able to envision or allow. In consequence, neither the practice of democracy, nor the fact of 'living in India', has been quite so unambiguously established in the case of the Northeast (or in Kashmir) as it might have been in other parts of the country: in these regions, the conflicts and unresolved tensions of 1947 might even appear to have been compounded over time. It is not surprising then that the charge of internal colonialism persists.

In other areas of India and amongst other disadvantaged groups, the discourse of an internal colonialism seems to have died out. What has hardly disappeared, however, is talk of marginalised groups and oppressed populations, the rights of minorities, democracy, equity and social justice. All of these have remained central to the arguments of the Indian nation and its politics.

I referred earlier to the Dalit-Bahujan claim (that is, the claim of the Dalits, the so-called Other Backward Castes and the religious minorities, together) of being 85 per cent of the people of India. Ironically, this claim exactly matches the Hindu right wing claim of representing, by their own calculation, 85 per cent of the people of the country. The challenge today is to see which of these assemblages is able to constitute itself into a new political majority, and thereby give a new content to democratic (or not so democratic) nationhood in India. Our hope must be that any such historically constituted majority will recognise its historicity, provisionality and changeability; will recognise that majorities, like nations, are not given but made, that today's minority may be tomorrow's majority, and that new minorities will arise to stake a claim to new majority positions.

If 'national' and 'democratic' continue to be the watchwords of the modern state, perhaps the time has come to downplay the 'national' element in the equation and underscore the democratic component, and to recognise that what has been crucial to the nationalist struggles of our time is not so much the claim of homogeneity and uniformity – one religion, one language, one culture, one nation – as the hope and expectation of democracy and development, human dignity and social justice. The fault lines of nationhood will appear very differently in such a light.

NOTES:

1   Benedict Anderson, *Imagined Communities: Reflections on the Origin and Spread of Nationalism* (London 1983); Partha Chatterjee, *Nationalism and the Colonial World. A Derivative Discourse?* (Delhi, 1986); Ernest Gellner, *Nations and Nationalism* (Oxford, 1983); Eric Hobsbawm, *Nations and Nationalism since 1870* (Cambridge, 1990); Elie Kedourie, *Nationalism* (London, 1960); Anthony D. Smith, *Theories of Nationalism* (London, 1971).

2   Jawaharlal Nehru, *The Discovery of India* (1946; Bombay 1961), pp.63, 147; and V.C. Joshi, ed., *Lala Lajpat Rai. Writings and Speeches, Volume Two, 1920-28* (Delhi, 1966), p.221.

3   *Vartman*, 12 October 1947.

4   In connection with the proposition that the 'language, appearance, religion, and practices' of the Muslims were 'all different' from those of the Hindus, I might note only that all the Indian Muslims I know or have heard of speak the Bengali, Gujarati, Marathi, Malayalam, Punjabi, Hindi, Urdu (or to break the vernaculars down further, the Awadhi, Bhojpuri, Magahi, etc.) of their regions. I should add that Urdu – designated the language of the Indian Muslims, which is also my language, and the language of very large numbers of Hindus and Sikhs of my parents' and grandparents' generation – whatever else it might be, is not a foreign language, but distinctively Indian (or, now, subcontinental). And just as

Indian intellectuals claim, with considerable justification, that English is now one of the languages of India, one would also have to assert that Islam is now (and has long been) one of the religions of India.

5   *Constituent Assembly Debates.* Vol. VIII, p.329.

6   Ambedkar and other Dalit leaders had of course already initiated a significant debate about the relevance of the category 'Hindu' for their followers, and similar questions had been raised in connection with the *adivasis* in the work of anthropologists, like, G.S. Ghurye and Verrier Elwin.

7   I should make it clear that while this attack obviously has something to do with the Muslim identity of the painter, that is not its stated ground. Muslim artisans and artists have contributed to Hindu festivals and prayers in significant ways: in Ayodhya, even today, the sacred wooden sandals worn by Hindu devotees and priests are often made by local Muslims.

8   *All Parties Conference 1928. Report of the Committee appointed by the Conference to determine the Principles of the Constitution for India* (Allahabad, 1928), p.27.

9   Theodore Morison, 'Muhammadan Movements,' in J. Cummings, ed., *Political India* (London, 1932).

10   'Pakistan' was not named in the Lahore Resolution, but, as Jinnah noted, press reports and the public response turned this into the 'Pakistan' resolution.

11   Latif Ahmed Sherwani, ed., *Pakistan Resolution to Pakistan, 1940-47. A Selection of Documents Presenting the Case for Pakistan* (Karachi, 1969, reprinted Delhi, 1985), p.36.

12   Interview with Viqar Ahmed, London, 15 October 1995.

13   M.A.H.Ispahani, 'Factors Leading to the Partition of British India', in C.H. Philips and M.D. Wainright, eds, *The Partition of India. Policies and Perspectives, 1935-1947* (London, 1970), p.350.

14   Cited in Ayesha Jalal, *The Sole Spokesman: Jinnah, the Muslim League, and the Demand for Pakistan* (Cambridge, 1985), p.263 (emphasis added).

15   See Leonard A. Gordon, 'Divided Bengal: Problems of Nationalism

and Identity in the 1947 Partition', in Mushirul Hasan, ed., *India's Partition. Process, Strategy and Mobilization* (Delhi, 1993), pp.297-98.

16   Ibid, p.307; and Jalal, *Sole Spokesman, pp.252 and 265.*

17   See, for example, the works by Mushirul Hasan, Ayesha Jalal cited in the preceding footnotes, and also my *Remembering Partition. Violence, Nationalism and History in India* (Cambridge, 2001), ch.2.

18   *The Statesman,* 23 November 1947.

19   Durga Das, ed., *Sardar Patel's Correspondence, 1945-50,* Vol.IV (Ahmedabad, 1972), p.421.

20   Ibid, p.422.

21   See my *Remembering Partition;* and for a detailed treatment of the Mevs, Shail Mayaram, *Resisting Regimes: Myth, Memory and the Shaping of a Muslim Identity* (Delhi, 1997).

22   David F. Pocock, *Kanbi and Patidar: A Study of the Patidar Community of Gujarat* (Oxford, 1972), p. 44.

23   Cf. Asghar Ali Engineer, *The Bohras,* (New Delhi, 1980); J.C. Masselos, 'The Khojas of Bombay', in Imtiaz Ahmad, ed., *Caste and Social Stratification among the Muslims* (Delhi, 1973).

24   For the recent Gujarat case, see Upendra Baxi's comments on 'cosmopolitan' versions of Gujarati *asmita,* 'The Second Gujarat Catastrophe', *Economic and Political Weekly* (24 August 2002), p.3523 and *passim;* for earlier comments on Ayodhya, Khalistan and other such battles, see S. Gopal, ed., *Anatomy of a Confrontation* (New Delhi, 1991); G. Pandey, ed., *Hindus and Others: the Question of Identity in India Today* (New Delhi, 1993); and Achin Vanaik, *The Furies of Indian Communalism : Religion, Modernity, and Secularization* (London, 1997).

25   There is no universally agreed name for the castes at the bottom of society whom I am concerned with here. Many are still referred to, and refer to themselves, by locally specific caste names – Chamar, Jatav, Pasi, Namasudra, Mahar, Mang, Nadar, etc. For long they were referred to collectively as outcastes, depressed castes (or classes) or Untouchables. Gandhi chose to describe them as

Harijans or children of God. The Government of India Act of 1935, and following that the Indian constitution of 1950, called them Scheduled Castes, in reference to a 'schedule' of the lowest castes that was drawn up in both documents. The chosen term of self-description by many of the most militant and outspoken of the ex-Untouchables is Dalit, which means the downtrodden or oppressed.

26   It is noteworthy that in India, which had more or less attained self-sufficiency in food production by the 1970s, the subsequent decades of globalisation and liberalisation have seen a recurrence of reports of large numbers of deaths from starvation. According to observers, the neglect of the rural poor was one of the reasons for the defeat of the BJP-led coalition government and its provincial allies in the last round of elections.

27   Of course, one has to qualify this further, to note that even the criminal law hardly applied equally to all of the subject population in colonial society. Caste, class and cultural privilege mattered here as in other spheres, and even theoretically the colonial ruling class was not always subject to the same laws as members of the colonized society.

28   These opinions are commonly expressed. For one example, see the statement of a Dalit activist cited in Partha Chatterjee, *The Politics of the Governed* (New Delhi 2004), p.25. The Dalit columnist, Chandrabhan Prashad, pushes the date of new opportunities further back, to the colonial period, putting the point in the following dramatic statement: 'The British came too late and left too early!'

29   See Ambedkar's writings of the 1940s, especially his *What Congress and Gandhi have done to the Untouchables* (Bombay, 1945).

30   Sekhar Bandhopadhyay, 'Transfer of Power and the Crisis of Dalit Politics in India, 1945-47', *Modern Asian Studies*, 34, 4 (2000), p. 903.

31   Ibid, p.906.

32 *Babasaheb Ambedkar's Writings and Speeches* (hereafter BAWS), Volume IX, pp. 181, 190; Volume XVII, pt 3, p.418; and Volume I, p.368

33 Ibid, p.376.

34 Ambedkar argued that these provisions for affirmative action should stay in place as long the condition of untouchability lasted, but had to settle for ten years; BAWS, XVII, 3, pp.420, 433. It is another matter that reservations have since been extended over and over again by ten-year periods.

35 BAWS.IX, p.68.

36 BAWS. XIV, pp.270-71.

37 Ibid, p.1162.

38 Eleanor Zelliot, *From Untouchable to Dalit. Essays on the Ambedkar Movement,* (Delhi, 1996), p.206.

39 BAWS, XVII, 3, p.536.

40 Bahujan Samaj Party slogans, cited in Zoya Hasan, 'Representation and Redistribution: the new lower caste politics of north India', in Francine Frankel, *et al,* eds, *Transforming India: Social and Political Dynamics of Democracy* (Delhi 2000), p.155 (my translation).

41 See *Kanshi Ram: Aaj ke neta. Aalochnatmak Adhyayanmala* (Delhi, 1996).

42 Cited in Abhay Kumar Dubey, 'Anatomy of a Dalit Power Player: A Study of Kanshi Ram', in Ghanshyam Shah, ed., *Dalit Identity and Politics* (Delhi, 2001), p.289.

43 BAWS, XVII, 3, p.214.

44 Sanjib Baruah, *India against Itself. Assam and the Politics of Nationality* (Philadelphia, 1999), title of ch.2.

45 See ibid, p.38.

46 Sanjoy Hazarika, *Strangers of the Mist, Tales of War and Peace from India's Northeast,* (New Delhi 1994), p.68.

47 Ibid, pp.97-98.

48 Sankaran Krishna, 'Cartographic Anxiety: Mapping the Body Politic in India', in Michael J. Shapiro & Hayward R. Walker, eds, *Challenging Boundaries: Global Flows, Territorial Identities* (Minneapolis, 1996), p.196.

49   Sanjoy Hazarika, *Strangers of the Mist*, p.63. The information
     on the distance to Hanoi and New Delhi also comes from this
     book; p. xv.

50   K. Saigal, former Planning and Development Commissioner of
     Assam, cited in Baruah, *India against Itself*, p.207.

51   Ibid., pp.207-08

pakistan: from minority rights to majoritarianism

in Pakistan, the conventional approach to understanding nationalism, in both its dominant and minority forms, is grounded in what may be called 'essentialist' interpretations of identity. Essentialist perspectives endow identity with supposedly objective qualities and see it as relatively fixed and unchanging across place and time. Essentialist evocations are not restricted to discourses about the nation and ethnicity but can equally include other categories of identity such as race, gender, class and sexuality.

In the literature on Pakistan, there are two major essentialist perspectives. The first is the dominant form of Pakistani nationalism or the 'two-nation' view, which claims that Muslims in colonial India were always an identifiable and separate community, that they always retained distinctive cultural traditions and were never assimilated into their Indian environment.[1] It is this essentialist notion of Muslim identity that underpins the search for a separate Muslim homeland and results in the crossing of the Rubicon of Partition. Once this essentialist view of community is adopted, the establishment of a separate state becomes a rational, logical and inevitable consequence.

Minorities in Pakistan have a very different perspective. They oppose the dominant official interpretation of nationalism and advance a counter-narrative that draws on the Marxist theory of nationality put forward by Stalin.[2] The Marxist definition equates nationality with language, and within Pakistan, Baluch and Sindhi activists have enthusiastically adopted this interpretation. In the 1970s, leading Baluch politicians, Ghaus Bux Bizenjo and Ataullah Mengal, argued on this basis for a multi-national federation with protection for the rights for minorities. Bizenjo's central argument was that the federal units of Pakistan consisted of separate nationalities and a strong centre would only emerge if it respected these rights.[3] This view, however, was rejected by the Pakistan government and its supporters. A. K. Brohi, a leading lawyer and protagonist of the 'two-nation' view, disingenuously argued that colonial India was never a federation based on nationality and that 'religion and religion alone… got together to form Pakistan … and the act is irrevocable and final'.[4]

Both of these essentialist perspectives are problematic, as they attempt to shoehorn awkward facts into their respective positions. The Baluch have to wrestle with the reality that two language groups – Brahui and Baluchi speakers – inhabit the same social space of Baluch identity and do not fit neatly into Stalin's thesis. In the case of Pakistani nationalism, no matter how hard they try, the two-nation theorists cannot erase the different language groups, provincial identities and sectarian differences within the Muslim population. In both cases, identity is not fixed spatially or temporally and the theories do not correspond neatly to realities. This example also illustrates the majority-minority conundrum, alluded to by Gyanendra Pandey, which is problematic for many nation-states.

An   alternative   approach,   which   challenges   these perspectives, is based on the theory of social constructionism. At the heart of the debate about identity, and in the social theory used to analyse it, is the recognition of 'Self', 'Other' and 'Us'. Nationalism, ethnicity and religion are identity-based categories that turn on the problem of self-recognition and recognition by others. Essentialist assertions are challenged by theories of social constructionism, which defy the notion that individuals or groups can have singular, integral, and unproblematic identities.[5] Rather they see nationalism, ethnicity, religious and other social movements as different points on a continuum of identity politics rather than as distinct and separate phenomena. A number of writers, notably Hobsbawn and Ranger,[6] Anderson,[7] Calhoun[8] and Hall,[9] systematically challenge the notion that nationalist or ethnic identifications are fixed across time or that nationalism grows out of or is based on ethnicity. They argue that an individual's loyalty to a collectivity is based on the 'imagining' of membership. In their view, it is this collective imagining, which may be reinforced by foundational myths, which establishes the subjective conditions that allow national groups to cohere.[10] However, imagining goes hand in hand with selective erasure of the past. Memories of forging the nation, in which brutality and bloodshed were required to physically batter and meld disparate groups together, are often erased from the collective narrative. Another important part of the imagining process is the construction of the 'Other', by which is meant those forces in opposition to which such groups define themselves. This is often linked to the role of war and conflict in constructing the boundary of the collectivity.[11] 'Otherisation' helps to define who its members are and assists in suppressing internal differences.

According to this approach, identity is contingent, contextual and not fixed in time or space; it is a dynamic notion, which can be imagined and re-imagined. Social constructionism permits an approach to social identity, which takes account of the complexity of different factors. It allows for a conceptual framework that can incorporate nationalism, ethnicity, religious identification or new ethnicities. It also helps us to understand the subjective dynamics operating among groups that aspire to establish discrete notions of community. This is a process that is subject to considerable internal discussion within such groups and constitutes an arena for momentous moral debate.[12]

Remembering and forgetting collective memories are indispensable parts of constructing group identities. However, this does raise the question: who decides what should be remembered or forgotten? For many analysts, identity politics has a class basis and specific actors make conscious decisions in pursuing their class interests, using cultural agendas and mobilisations. Hamza Alavi, in his influential work on Pakistani nationalism, identified what he called the 'salariat' as particularly important in this process. According to his view, the salariat, a fraction of the middle class, reflects the interests not only of educated professionals in 'white collar employment, notably in the state apparatus, but also those who aspire to such jobs'.[13] The service class are functionaries occupying positions in the national or provincial bureaucracy and their employability is restricted or expanded by the recognition of particular languages by the nation-state. For the educated population in rural and agricultural society, the primary source of employment and advancement comes from government occupations. The upper echelons of the administration, senior bureaucrats and military officers, have a qualitatively different status from lower level functionaries, but share a common desire and struggle for access to limited opportunities and resources. In this struggle for state resources, the salariat reconstitutes itself and fractures along ethnic lines, reflecting uneven regional development, occupational specialisations by communities, as well as historical divisions of labour. It is an auxiliary class, playing an indispensable role in identity politics – nationalist, ethnic or communal – alongside other classes, which may include the urban petty bourgeoisie, small traders and businessmen. These '*bazaaris*' play an important role in identity-based politics and mobilise behind the salariat in order to compete with more established communities. Other classes, such as aspiring members of the salariat from the landowning classes, prosperous peasants or skilled labourers, use education to access government employment and are linked to the salariat through organic bonds of kinship and village ties. In this way, the salariat is able to mobilise wide community support for its demands. Local power holders may jump on the bandwagon, as demands for regional autonomy dovetail with the political ambitions of influential landlords and tribal leaders. These class interests gain from the politics of nationalism and regionalism, while the subordinate classes, the working class and the peasantry, have much less to gain from identity-based mobilisations.[14]

One weakness of the theory of social constructionism is that it minimises the role of political structure in shaping national and other movements. Structure can be comprehended in a number of ways: it can be the power of state institutions and the monopoly of violence they enjoy or it can be the power that emanates from knowledge and the influence this has on shaping people's consciousness. State power is important in producing collective identities – both because it can be used to construct a national identity and because it can provoke processes of resistance based on alternative identities. The French political thinker, Foucault, makes the case that power is not restricted to political institutions. In his famous work, *Discipline and Punish*, he argues that knowledge and power are integrated in a productive set of connections running through society.[15] Knowledge produces what he calls 'discourse', or theories of knowledge, which transform the individual consciousness and shape belief systems and world views. Education and the media are the most significant ways the state structure attempts to modulate and change such world views. Tariq Rahman calls this 'pragmatic power'[16] and highlights the importance of the usage of language in the bureaucracy, military, judiciary, media, educational system and business corporations. Access to state power depends on being proficient in the language used in these institutions and those people who are naturally conversant in this language due to expensive education or birth have an obvious advantage over those who are not so privileged.

As far as the salariat is concerned – whether at national or provincial level – access to power in the state apparatus is dependent on its language being recognised and used as a state language. In Pakistan, for example, competing nationalist visions put forward by different ethnic groups are usually predicated on the assumption that statehood or regional autonomy will privilege their particular language at the expense of competing groups. Language, explicitly or implicitly, is critical for the salariat's ambitions in identity politics, and the educational system that produces adepts in a particular language is equally crucial. In short, identity politics is about pragmatic power and the cultural recognition of groups by the state.

The nation-state is an instrument of power, which systematically monopolises violence to maintain control over its territory.[17] In relation to managing internal difference, nation-states adopt two broad approaches: either to eliminate difference or to manage it. Erasure of difference in the nineteenth century was not merely considered to be an acceptable price to pay for nationhood but was celebrated as the path to progress. John Stuart Mill denigrates the aspirations of smaller cultures and nationalities and expresses the unshakeable belief that progress requires their assimilation into larger national entities. 'Nobody can suppose that it is not more beneficial to a Breton, or Basque of French Nevarra, to be brought into the current of ideas and feelings of a highly civilised and cultivated people – to be a member of the French nationality ... than to sulk on his rocks, the half savage relic of past times, revolving in his own little mental orbit, without participation or interest in the general movement of the world.'[18] Similarly, Marx and Engels accepted the emergence and unification of great nations in Europe. They supported their advancement in the case of France, Italy, Poland and Germany and their independence in the case of England, Hungary, Spain and Russia, but rejected the idea that smaller nationalities such as the Czechs, Croats, Basques, Welsh, Bulgarians, Romanians and Slovenes had any such rights. Smaller nationalities were expected to assimilate into one of the great nations without their cultural and linguistic characteristics being recognised. Engels argued that 'this ethnic trash always become fanatical standard bearers of counter revolution and remain so until their complete extirpation or loss of their national character'.[19] The consequence of this kind of thinking was genocide, forced mass-population transfer, partition or assimilation, which quite often provoked secessionist movements and ethnic resistance.

This nineteenth century approach to nation building has a strong resonance within the Pakistani state. Partition, which involved in Punjab the erasure of difference though ethnic cleansing, was how the states of India and Pakistan were born. Extreme measures were also used by the Pakistani state in its attempts to erase Bangladeshi and Baluch separatism. However erasure, through genocide and ethnic cleansing, is far more difficult to accomplish in the twenty-first century because the international community is more vigilant and sometimes willing to intervene.

Alternatively, nation-states can attempt to manage difference by negotiation. Federalism is a common mechanism for managing difference in multi-lingual states and it can be successful in regulating ethnic conflict if the boundaries between ethnic communities match the units of the federation. In countries like India and Nigeria, federations emerged out of multi-ethnic colonies, where administrative elites had an interest in sustaining the federation and where it could be justified in terms of large economic markets and greater security. One attraction of a federal system is that it allows regulation of ethnic difference without the resort to coercion.[20] However, the federalist rationale in post-colonial states has frequently been inverted. In South Asia in particular, the argument that strong federal governments are necessary to corral diverse pluralities into the nation has often disguised ulterior motives. As Gowher Rizvi puts it: 'Denial of autonomy to regional and particularist groups is often a ploy for internal imperialism'.[21] The key to India's relative success in maintaining its diversity and heterogeneity has been through accommodation. India's formal democracy, combined with the formation of linguistic states, 'regional political economies and electoral processes', has allowed for greater resistance to central interference. There have been some obvious exceptions to this generalisation, but compared to Pakistan, the margins for centre-state negotiations are much greater, while the greater degree of centralisation found in Pakistan leaves far less room for manoeuvre. In Pakistan, the options are difficult choices 'of cooperation on the centre's terms or costly anti-state defiance'.[22]

I now propose to look at three important historical periods in the development of Pakistani nationalism. These three periods witnessed contending visions of nationalism and precipitated political crises, which shaped the future of the country. They are firstly, the years running up to partition and independence in 1947; secondly, the break-up of Pakistan and the emergence of an independent Bangladesh in 1971; and thirdly, the more recent emergence of a distinct Mohajir ethnicity among those who were earlier the chief protagonists of Pakistani nationalism. What I hope to show is how Muslim nationalism evolved and mutated in different historical periods, how new identities were imagined and constructed, and how different factors – of culture, agency and structure – contributed to this process.

the rise of muslim nationalism

Muslim nationalism, as it emerged in the 1940s, is a good example of identity politics mobilising around cultural markers and idioms, based on language and religion, to contest the claims of Indian nationalism in the run-up to independence and partition. In the imagining of Muslim nationalism, erasure of collective memory was an important element, as we see in Ishtiaq Hussain Qureshi's teleology of a distinct Muslim identity in the distant past, which ignores evidence that Muslim identification was always highly contested and ambiguous.[23] In India before 1947, both elites and masses were steeped in hybrid practices that emerged from the inter-reaction between Islamic and local cultures and languages. The suppression of the hybrid dimension of Indo-Persian culture, which had been the dominant cultural norm in North India for more than 200 years, and the exclusive emphasis on the Islamic dimension, was part of the remembering and forgetting process.

In the late nineteenth century, there was widespread surprise at the number of Muslims that were recorded in the early censuses. It challenged a popular misconception held by the British and by non-Muslims that the Muslim population was primarily composed of invaders and immigrants and was concentrated in relatively small numbers around centres of power. In fact, most Muslims were converts as a result of the missionary activities of *pirs,* who developed a hybrid blend of popular religion, based on religious psychology, tolerance and the cultivation of transcendental experiences drawing on yogic and tantric traditions. The intercessionary role of Muslim saints in answering prayers and their tolerance of traditional customs and practices, such as laws of inheritance or beliefs in deities, found an attentive audience among the illiterate and those unwilling to endure theological rigour.[24]

Cultural hybridity was expressed in literature, architecture, music and language. Translations of Hindu classics, such as the Ramayana and Mahabharata, or musical theory such as *Ragdarpan*, took place from Sanskrit into Persian. In architecture and painting, there was a delicate blending of Muslim styles and techniques with Hindu traditions and content. Mughal buildings reflected the blending of vaulted arches, domes and courtyards, with Indian traditions of solidity and ornate embellishment. In painting, there was a synthesis of Iranian composition style and subject matter with animals and plants drawn from Hindu mythology.[25]

It was the emergence of Urdu as the hybrid language of court culture that bequeathed the lasting legacy. It is generally believed that Urdu originated as a mixture of old Punjabi and Persian and that when Muslim rule expanded to Delhi it was *Khari Boli,* a variety of Hindi, that provided the grammatical structure around which Persian vocabulary was added. The distinctly Indic sound system found in all Indo-Aryan languages was preserved, but many Persian and Arabic words were naturalised, and this introduced new sounds previously lacking in Indic languages. As Muslim rule expanded from Delhi in the thirteenth and early fourteenth century, Urdu was carried eastward as a secondary language of communication, along with the officially used Persian, without the displacement of local languages. This situation remained throughout the Mughal period, with Persian as the language of state and Urdu the popular medium of communication. It was not until the mid-eighteenth century that

Urdu supplanted Persian as the language of court business and literary and cultural interest. This was the age of Khwaja Mir Dard, Mirza Rafi Saud and Mir Taqi Mir in Awadh,[26] decrying the decay of empire and of cultured society in an Urdu that had much of its popular Hindi vocabulary displaced by Persian idioms and metaphors.

From the late nineteenth century onwards, Muslim and Hindu elites became involved in re-interpreting the past, erasing memories of hybrid cultural manifestations and re-inventing history to construct essentialist communities around faith. The fuzzy boundaries of Muslim identity became arenas of political contestation and the subject of religious reform.[27] Religious revival movements by Muslims and non-Muslims rewrote the hybrid tradition. The censuses of the late nineteenth century alerted religious groups to the fact that there were numbers of people who exhibited hybrid religious characteristics. The Arya Samaj in Punjab and the Hindu Mahasabha in Hardwar initiated *shuddhi* (mass purification) and conversion movements of low-caste Hindus (Rahtias, Odhs, Meghs and Jats) and of Hindu converts to Islam (Malkana Rajput, Gujjar and Bania). In due course, this process, which has come to be known as Sanskritisation, was accompanied by *sangathan,* or the unification of various Hindu groups into a dominant pan-Hindu revivalist framework.

Among the Muslims, the search for religious authenticity was initiated in the eighteenth century by Shah Walliullah, who concluded that the decline of Muslim dynasties was due to their deviation from the true path. The two main culprits he identified were the popularity of Shiahism among the Muslim elite (with its more relaxed sexual code and its allowance of temporary marriage) and the non-Muslim influences that were incorporated by the Sufis into their practices. His influence contributed to the revivalist trend in Islam, which eventually led to the emergence of the reformist *madrassah* at Deoband. His ideas were also influential in non-elite movements such as the Tariqah-i-Muhammediyah Movement, which initiated an anti-British Islamisation process in rural Bengal, accusing hybrid cults of *shirk* (polytheism) and *bid'ah* (sinful innovation). However, it was the *shuddhi* and *sangathan* campaign of the 1920s (started by Hindu activists in the wake of the Khilafat Movement) that prompted Muslims to initiate similar programmes, such as *tabligh* (propaganda) and *tanzim* (organisation), and accentuated these revivalist trends. [28]

Politicians reinforced the message that hybrid identifications were not only religiously unacceptable but also a political liability. The introduction of the census had highlighted religious and caste divisions within Indian society and the terms on which constitutional reforms were introduced in India in the nineteenth and twentieth centuries politicised some of these divisions. The colonial authorities allocated resources, education and employment, and seats in the legislatures on the basis of the numerical strength of respective communities. Hybrid cultural practices did not fit neatly into this system of categorisation, which required groups to belong to clearly defined, religious communities. Many Muslim political leaders based their authority on an unproblematic notion of community. Once separate electorates had been introduced, they only had to appeal to their fellow Muslims and could then make extravagant claims without the fear of alienating other voters. In this process, religious and caste identities became highly politicised, marking a clear break from the past, where hybrid cultural practices were much more widespread and customary.[29]

the history of the muslim salariat

Muslim society was socially deeply divided with pronounced caste and class divisions compounded by linguistic variations.

Persian had been the language of courtly business (of both Muslim and non-Muslim rulers), but it was in decline by the eighteenth century among the *Ashraf* elite. It was gradually displaced by Urdu, which became the lingua franca of northern India, Gujarat and the Deccan. The majority of Muslims, however, learned first the local language – Punjabi, Bengali, Gujarati, Malayalam or Tamil[30] – and the use of Urdu was an uneven process and varied from region to region. This was all to change with the anglicisation of the state by the British. Thomas B. Macaulay's famous minute replaced Persian with English as the business language of the executive and judiciary and introduced the vernacular in the lower echelons of the bureaucracy. The other impact of the anglicising process was on the Muslim clergy or *ulama*, who previously taught the Ashraf elite Arabic and Persian in their madrassahs. Anglicisation resulted in the demise of the Persian/Arabic salariat, as the student demand for this form of education dried up. The introduction of statute law in English replaced *shariah* law and removed the *ulama* from the legal function they had performed in the past. There now emerged a clear difference between the Muslim elite, who spoke English, and the middle classes, who spoke vernacular languages.[31]

By the early twentieth century, members of the Muslim elite were educated in English, just like their non-Muslim counterparts. Muhammad Ali Jinnah and Jawaharlal Nehru had more in common with each other than with their co-religionists, as they were both more at ease in English than in Urdu or Hindi. The English-educated Muslim elite was quite happy to work with Indian nationalism, particularly in its constitutional phase, but had to carry with it the support of the vernacular speaking Muslim middle class or salariat, which was greatly concerned by the decline of Urdu as the language of governance.

The replacement of Persian by English and vernacular languages had immediate implications for Urdu-speakers in

North India because it raised the issue of whether Persianised Urdu might be replaced by Hindi. While the elites from all communities competed for employment opportunities requiring a command of English, the salariat competed for opportunities that existed in the vernacular. Use of a specific vernacular facilitated the entry of particular groups into government employment and the demand in North India that Urdu be replaced as the language of government by Hindi in the Devanagari script was not only a sign of Hindu assertiveness but a clear threat to Muslim employment. Muslims in the United Provinces represented only 12 per cent of the population but they were heavily urbanised and were represented above their percentage of the population in the professions. In 1857, they held 64 per cent of posts in the subordinate judicial and executive service (higher ranks were reserved for the British) but by 1886, this had been reduced to 45 per cent.[32] The substitution of Urdu had a severe impact on Muslim fortunes and induced an overwhelming feeling of cultural loss and a sense that their way of life was in jeopardy.

It was at this time, in the midst of the Urdu-Hindi controversy, that Sir Sayed Ahmad Khan started talking and writing of separatism. The Anjuman-i-Taraqqi-i-Urdu was set up to defend Urdu and to challenge the Hindi Sahitya Sammelan and its supporters in the Congress. The fact that Urdu was the vernacular used in the Punjab and areas under its control, like the North-West Frontier and British Baluchistan, meant that Muslims from the United Provinces were able to mobilise a wider body of middle-class opinion on this issue. The Urdu-Hindi language controversy, however, was not a major issue in Bengal or Sindh, as Urdu was not the vernacular used by the authorities in those regions.

The defence of Islam was also linked to the defence of Urdu. The Hindu demand for cow protection and for the right to play music in front of mosques, even during prayers, was perceived as part of a wider onslaught against Muslim culture and the Muslim way of life. Hindu revivalist organisations, in particular the Arya Samaj and Sanatan Dharma Sabha, demanded cow protection and agitated for legislation that would restrict the use of slaughterhouses and kebab shops. In some cases, there was forcible interference with the sale and slaughter of cows and sabha courts were set up, that punished sellers of cows to butchers.

The Islamisation process taking place among Muslims produced a complex response to this Hindu assertiveness. Efforts to curb cow slaughter were rebuffed by Muslim insistence that *Bakr-Eid* sacrifices were crucial for Islamic ritual, often making the issue more explosive and leading to violence. Simultaneously, revivalist currents were becoming sectarian and Shiahs and Ahmadiyyas became the target of Sunni revivalists. In Punjab in the 1930s, the Ahrars, a militant Sunni Muslim organisation, became involved in a struggle with the heterodox Ahmadiyyas, while among Sunnis and Shiahs across North India controversy over the recitation of *tabarra* (the Shiah practice of denigrating the first three caliphs of Islam) disturbed the notion of a monolithic Muslim community. All the sectarian fault lines that became so active in Pakistan were present in the late 1930s.[33]

This did not mean, however, that the *ulama* favoured Muslim separatism. In fact, some influential *ulama* had a history of cooperation with Indian nationalism. After the First World War, these divines formed the Jamiat-ul-Ulama-i-Hind (JUH) and launched the Khilafat Movement at the behest of Gandhi in tandem with the Non-Cooperation Movement. Post-Khilafat, the JUH, the Ahrars, the Muslim Majlis and other revivalist groups maintained an ambivalent relationship with Muslim nationalism. They were not sympathetic to the separatist implication of the Lahore Resolution and were concerned about the fate of Muslims that would be left behind in India. Maulana Hussain Ahmad Madani, the senior divine of the JUH, castigated the two-nation theory as divisive and playing into the hands of British imperialism. The JUH remained loyal throughout to the Congress, and the Muslim League only gained some support from the *ulama,* when a breakaway faction formed the Jamiat-ul-Ulama-i-Islam. Even as late as 1946, many of the Deobandi, Brelvi and Ahl-i-Hadith *ulama* remained loyal to Indian nationalism.

Once the Muslim elite began to move along a different path from Indian nationalism, their dilemma was how to forge a unified constituency from this disparate and diverse community, with conflicting interests, spread across the length and breadth of India. Their answer was to develop a minority rights discourse, which attempted to fuse these disparate groups behind real and imagined grievances. They embarked on a process of political mobilisation, by using arguments of relative deprivation and by highlighting threats to Muslim culture, economic interests and employment prospects in an independent India under Congress rule. However, while relative deprivation was an issue in Bengal and some Muslim-majority provinces, it was not an issue in the United Provinces, where despite being in a minority, the Muslim elite was relatively wealthy and influential.

The minority rights discourse drew on a number of existing themes, invented others and tried to advance an agenda that was universal to the interest of the Muslim salariat. However, the task of unifying a disparate group, divided by language, sectarian difference, social class and caste as well as custom and practice, under the banner of religion nearly proved to be insurmountable. It was a contested identification in the Muslim-minority United Provinces, Bihar, Gujarat and Central Provinces as well as in Muslim-majority provinces of Bengal, the Punjab, the North-West Frontier Province and Sindh. Consequently, to overcome the divisive nature of Muslim politics the strategy that emerged was not to define in detail the content of Muslim nationalism but to emphasise the threat from the 'Other'.

The opportunity for such an approach did not really appear until after the 1937 elections, when Muslim League-Congress negotiations broke down over the terms for forming a coalition in the United Provinces. Up to this point, the legacy of the Lucknow Pact of 1916, reinforced by cooperation between the communities during the Khilafat Movement, had exercised a powerful influence on both the Muslim League and the Congress. It was this understanding which underlined the expectation of Muslim Leaguers in the United Province that they would enter into a coalition in the provincial government. The Congress, however, emboldened by its own success and the poor showing nationally of the Muslim League, took a tough stand in the negotiations and was only prepared to offer the U.P. Muslim League positions in the U.P. provincial government if it would accept merger with the Congress Party.[34]

After this, the Muslim elite in the Muslim-minority provinces was faced with multiple assaults against its political and economic interests. Its power base in the United Provinces was threatened by the land reforms of the Govind Ballabh Pant ministry and the Muslim Mass Contact Campaign launched by the Congress Party was seen as an attempt to erode its political constituency and marginalise it further. The lack of organic links between the Ashraf elite and the Muslim masses limited severely the options that were available. Adopting a communal strategy overcame these serious difficulties by targeting the Hindus as the 'Other'.

The 'Otherisation' of the Congress Party as a Hindu Party became a clear campaign tactic when the League raised the 'Islam in Danger' slogan in the Bundelkhand by-election.[35] By reinforcing existing concerns of Congress dominance, the League was able to co-opt communalist parties: the United Party of

Bihar, Muslim Parliamentary Party of the Central Provinces, the Ittihad-i-Millat of the Punjab and the National Agricultural Party of the United Provinces. It also entered into alliance with non-League parties in the Muslim majority provinces by means of the Sikander-Jinnah pact in the Punjab and a similar agreement with Fazlul Huq in the Bengal.[36]

The strategy of widening the gap between communities resulted in an increase in communal tensions and fierce clashes in Allahabad and Benares in 1938. This tension was aggravated by Congress-led peasant mobilisations against Muslim landlords.[37] The Muslim League then published a series of reports accusing Congress governments of 'atrocities' and systematic 'discrimination'. The Pirpur Report and several others lambasted the Congress for a systematic attack on Muslim identity and singled out the Mass Muslim Contact Campaign, the Wardha education programme, the singing of *Bande Matram* and the use of Hindi in the administration.[38] The political nature of these accusations was demonstrated by Jinnah's refusal to accept a judicial investigation by Sir Maurice Gwyer, Chief Justice of the Federal Court.[39] As Khaliquzzaman stated to Governor Hallet of the United Provinces: 'the charges against Hindu Congress Governments are not proved or not wholly proved' but there was a perceived threat.[40] While there was an issue concerning the use of Hindi, most of the charges in these reports were aimed at constructing an essentialised Muslim identity in opposition to the Congress Party, which was treated as synonymous with the Hindu 'Other'. This Muslim League strategy was most successful in the United Provinces, Bihar and Bengal. It was, however, unable to dislodge the Muslim-Sikh coalition in the Punjab led by the Unionist Party; it had little impact on the Red Shirts and their alliance with the Congress in the North-West Frontier; and remained peripheral to politics in Sindh and Baluchistan or in the princely states.

re-imagining the muslim nation

The main promoters of Muslim nationalism were Muslims from the minority provinces and particularly the United Provinces; the Punjabi Muslims, followed by the Bengali Muslims, were only converted to the cause with real difficulty. How best to protect Muslim political, economic and cultural interests was a difficult and intractable problem, considering the considerable internal diversity of the all-India Muslim community. In nationalist hagiographies there is an unproblematic path from the conceptualisation of the Pakistan idea to its realisation as a separate and independent state. Mohammad Iqbal provided the inspiration. Chaudhuri Rahmat Ali invented the acronym. This was crystallised in the Lahore Resolution of 1940, which became the goal of the Muslim League: an independent homeland. The reality was far more complex. There was considerable intellectual ferment throughout the 1930s and 1940s over the future of the Muslims and there were a number of ideas that were gaining popularity at that time. These were separatist, federal or confederal in nature. Rahmat Ali was *persona non-grata* with the Muslim League, as he had clashed with Jinnah over the idea in the 1930s and hurled abuse at him when the separatist option was rejected.[41] The animosity between the old guard of the Muslim League and the inventor of the Pakistan slogan was so deep that it continued even after independence, when Liaquat Ali, the country's first prime minister, urged him to leave Pakistan or face reprisals. Rahmat Ali's body lies to this date in a humble grave in Cambridge and his well-wishers have been repeatedly refused permission to rebury him in the country that he named. However, Rahmat Ali's Pakistan National Movement was influential, particularly in the Punjab among Muslim League supporters, and the slogan was co-opted by the League for its mobilising capacity. In spite of Jinnah's distaste for it, he was forced to back down on this issue.[42]

The Pakistan slogan's real significance was that it prompted a major debate among Muslims on their political future. The Aligarh scheme subsequently refined Rahmat Ali's separatist proposal to accommodate a minority-province viewpoint and this in turn provoked federalist responses. One federalist blueprint, first initiated by Khwaja Iqbal, was re-shaped by Sikander Hayat, the premier of the Punjab, who produced two versions (both were aimed at preventing partition of that province). Another was put forward by Sayed Abdul Latif in his zonal scheme, which had the princely states in mind. Kiyafat Ali, with the encouragement of Jinnah, responded with a confederal option that attempted to satisfy the conflicting interests of Muslims without going down the road of separatism.[43]

Within the Muslim League there was considerable reluctance to sign up to the Lahore Resolution because it was promoted by the Punjab. All the intractable ethnic fault lines that emerged in Pakistan were apparent in response to the resolution and all leaders of ethnic movements within Pakistan – most notably Mujibur Rahman with his famous 'six points' – have justified their resistance to the centre on that basis. The Resolution states:

'The Government of India Act, 1935, is altogether unacceptable to Muslim India. ... No constitutional plan would be workable ... or acceptable to the Muslims unless it is designed on the following basic principles, viz., that geographically contiguous units are demarcated into regions which should be so constituted, with such territorial readjustments as may be necessary, that the areas in which the Muslims are numerically in a majority, as in the north-western and eastern zone of India, should be grouped to constitute "Independent States" of which the constituent units shall be autonomous and sovereign.'[44]

The draft resolution put forward by Sikander Hayat was based on his federal scheme. This elicited a number of responses from the drafting committee, which radically transformed the document. First Bengal, led by Shaheed Suhrawardy, put up enormous resistance to any mention of a centre to make the resolution acceptable to that province. References to a centre were dropped and the resolution stated that there would be two independent states, as Bengal was not prepared to be roped into a single state structure.[45] It was only after the 1946 elections, when Jinnah convened the Muslim League Legislators' Convention in preparation for the Cabinet Mission, that all references to two states were dropped. By then Jinnah was at the height of his authority and Suhrawardy and Abul Hashim of Bengal were reluctant to oppose him, even though they disagreed with the new formulation.[46] The reference to 'contiguous units' being 'demarcated into regions' was inserted due to lobbying from Liaquat Ali Khan. He wanted to avoid the word 'provinces', so that areas within Muslim minority provinces would also be covered by the resolution.[47] Finally, the wording that constituent units would be autonomous and sovereign was designed to allay the fears of Sindh and NWFP who did not want to be bundled into a 'zone' with the Punjab. Both Sindh and NWFP had campaigned hard for provincial status and were not going to let this hard fought autonomy be lost.

In Sindh's case, the argument for separation from Bombay Presidency had been couched in terms of the linguistic, cultural and economic distinctiveness of the region. This ethnic distinctiveness was also expressed in Sindh's opposition to the settlement of Punjabis in the Jamrao Canal colony, which prompted fears of it being absorbed by its larger neighbour. Sindhi identity had been constructed in opposition to the Bombay presidency and to the Punjab, and the 1940 Resolution had to address these concerns before bringing Sindhis on board.[48] In NWFP, Pukhtun ethnicity had been a major strand in the demand for provincial autonomy and this was constructed around the Pashto language and *pukhtunwali* (the tribal code).

Like the Sindhis, the Pukhtuns were not prepared to submerge their ethnic distinctiveness in a north-western zone.[49]

The Foreign Committee of the All-India Muslim League met several times to flesh out the Lahore Resolution but was unable to reach a conclusion from the array of proposals that were considered. Finally, the committee recommended the establishment of two separate states, but its report remained unpublished. When the Sindhi political leader, Abdullah Haroon, later leaked the report, it was immediately repudiated by Jinnah.[50] Such divisions continued to make agreement on future policy very difficult. When Jinnah convened a National Planning Committee to decide on development plans for Pakistan, the committee was unable to make any detailed recommendations without a prior understanding of the status of Pakistan. Was it to be a separate entity or to exist within some form of Indian polity?[51]

Jinnah's ambivalence was because he anticipated the adverse reaction that defining Pakistan would cause among his supporters. It would have opened up the very same fault lines which were to appear once Pakistan was established. Certainly in the Punjab and Bengal, separation implied partition of those provinces, which was an unacceptable price and explains the number of alternatives that emanated from there. Separatism also offered little to Muslim interests in the princely states. The most ardent and vocal supporters of separatism came from the United Provinces but even they envisaged the establishment of Muslim enclaves and not the migration of population.[52]

These debates, initiated by Muslims in Punjab and the minority provinces, triggered similar discussions in Bengal. There Fazlul Huq led the demand for an independent state and the *Purba* Pakistan movement argued for a Greater Bengal and opposed those who were ready to partition the province.[53] One theme was common among the cacophony of ideas: all the different Muslim protagonists wanted a high degree of decentralisation or regional autonomy with limited interference from the centre. Some believed this objective could only be realised by setting up a separate, independent state but the majority were not in favour of partition and wanted to stay within a larger political entity. The strength of this anti-separatist element can be gauged by the reaction within the Muslim League when partition was announced.

In this phase, Muslim nationalism was a loose coalition of conflicting class interests and linguistic groups that in a very broad fashion attempted to represent the Muslim interest in India. The prime instigators of the Pakistan movement were the Muslim-minority provinces, in particular the United Provinces, with the Punjab and Bengal playing influential and sometimes contradictory roles. However, there was no unity of vision among these major players of Muslim nationalism. Even though Muhammad Ali Jinnah presented Pakistan within a 'two-nation' discourse, it was clear that this was more political rhetoric than substance. When he was faced with the agonising decision of accepting a truncated Pakistan through partition, he clearly preferred the Cabinet Mission Plan, in which Pakistan would have been a federation within a confederation. Liaquat Ali Khan went so far as to suggest that if the Cabinet Mission Plan was renamed the Mountbatten Plan, it would stand an incomparably better chance of being accepted by the League.[54] Many of Jinnah's staunchest supporters from the United Provinces, such as the Raja of Mahmudabad and Hasrat Mohani, preferred to remain in their ancestral homes rather than migrate to Pakistan.[55] The Punjab Muslim League was paralysed with shock, as most of the leadership came from territory ceded to India.[56] The Bengal leadership, led by Shaheed Suhrawardy, made a last ditch attempt to negotiate with Sarat Chandra Bose for an independent United Bengal.[57] Jinnah saw this as a means to avoid partition, which would encourage other provinces and princely states to demand independence and foil the Congress intention of establishing a centralised state.[58]

Conventional understandings of Pakistani nationalism argue that in this period Muhammad Ali Jinnah shifted positions and adopted the two-nation thesis. I have argued instead that he was not a dyed in the wool separatist and that his pronouncements on the two-nation thesis were for political consumption. Actions speak louder than words and when he was offered what he called 'a truncated and moth-eaten Pakistan', he rejected it, preferring to remain within a loose Indian political entity. What this suggests is that Muslim nationalism was essentially a minority rights discourse and that the Muslim League remained ready even in 1946 to remain in the Indian union. Jinnah's supporters were shocked by Partition and even the most ardent separatists from the minority provinces found it very difficult, if not traumatic, to migrate to the country they had founded. Independent Pakistan emerged because of the exigencies of the transfer of power and the raging communal violence that erupted at that time. It brought with it new opportunities for the educated middle class, which had supported the Muslim League campaign and became the salariat of the new state. However, it also contained unresolved contradictions which were to make the imagining of Pakistani nationalism a very contested process.

the emergence of bangladesh

This section will take a snapshot of the re-imagining process, which led first to tension within Pakistan nationalism and ultimately to the break-up of the country. The partition of India and the establishment of Pakistan resulted in a process of erasure and re-imagining of identity within all the nationalist and ethnic currents in the country. The biggest change was in Muslim nationalism, which had earlier championed a minority rights discourse, defending the Urdu language and Islam, and demanding decentralisation of power. With the establishment of Pakistan, it dropped many of these demands and argued instead for a centralised unitary state, paying only lip service to Islam and the Urdu language. An important factor in explaining this somersault was the impact of Partition on the leadership of the Muslim League. The most active proponents of the Pakistan idea were from the Muslim-minority provinces, in particular the United Provinces, or from Muslim-minority regions of Punjab, which became part of India. After 1947, this Mohajir and Punjabi leadership, including Jinnah, found that they had established a nation-state in which they had no political constituency. Liaquat Ali Khan, who hailed from the United Provinces, was nominated to represent a constituency from East Bengal in the Constituent Assembly. Overall, the senior ranks of the Muslim League leadership found that they had no political base in the land to which they had migrated. For the Urdu speaking and Punjabi migrant leadership, this was a serious dilemma and their solution (in order to consolidate Pakistan and retain their dominance) was to work in a top-down fashion: to create a strong centralised state, with themselves firmly entrenched, and then establish political roots.[59] The whole exercise was given urgency by the troubled relations with India over the division of state assets, the disputed succession in Hyderabad and Junagadh, fighting over Kashmir and the disruptive killing and violence which accompanied Partition. Jinnah had already assumed the position of Governor General and had the powers required to deal with these crises. But the fact that he, as political leader of the Muslim League, had decided to take these powers set a dangerous precedent for authoritarian rule in the longer term.[60]

Erasure of the past also affected the Islamic parties. The majority of them had supported Indian nationalism but many now found themselves in Pakistan and had to reformulate their position. The reactions of Islamic parties to the constitution-making process and the agitations by the Jamaat-i-Islami over Kashmir, or by the Ahrars against the Ahmadiyya sect in Punjab, were attempts to establish their credentials among their new political constituencies. Ethnic parties, particularly those that were associated with Indian nationalism, such as the Khudai Khidmatgars, were also obliged to re-interpret the past to establish their credibility in a country they had opposed.

constructing the pakistani nation

Though the majority normally rules in a democracy, in the state of Pakistan this practice was turned on its head, with a minority holding on to the reigns of power at the centre and trying to rule the majority. Throughout Pakistan's early years, the Bengalis in the Eastern wing of the country, who constituted a majority of the population of the new state, were seen as a threat to the ruling elite in West Pakistan, who made strenuous efforts to keep them out of power. For this reason, in the 1950s, there was a shift from the minority rights discourse of the pre-independence period to a discourse of parity between the two wings. This tried to offset the numerical superiority of East Pakistan by creating a new administrative unit in West Pakistan with equal powers and representation.

The country's first constitution established a unitary structure that was secular in nature, and gave formal recognition to Urdu as the state language. Early constitutional formulations gave Islam only a superficial role, as Prime Minister Liaquat Ali was only willing to admit it in the naming of Pakistan as an Islamic republic and in a reference in the preamble that the laws would be in conformity with the Quran and the *Sunnah*.[61] This provoked a massive political controversy and constitutional deadlock. The Basic Principles Report drew criticism from the religious parties, as they wanted a constitutional role for the *ulama* to vet legislation for compatibility with Islam. The humiliating dismissal of the Bengali Prime Minister, Khwaja Nazimuddin, by the military-bureaucratic oligarchy in 1953 was to prevent him from making substantive concessions to the *ulama*.[62] The 1956 Constitution devised by President Iskander Mirza resisted giving any such concession to the religious parties and included only a perfunctory recognition of Islam. President Ayub Khan's constitution of 1962 attempted even to drop the term 'Islamic' but was forced to retreat on this issue by a religious backlash. Again there was no substantive role for the *ulama* in ensuring the compatibility of legislation and laws with the *Quran* and *Sunnah*.

The second contentious aspect of the constitution-making process was the demand by the minority provinces of West Pakistan, led by East Pakistan, for a decentralised polity as well as the recognition of Bengali as a state language. The desire for a decentralised federation was so strong that these provinces were prepared to work for better relations with India and thus negate the call for a larger army. Simultaneously, they attempted to use the political process to translate their numerical majority into institutional predominance. This tension was at the heart of the constitutional crisis of 1954, which resulted in the dissolution of the Constituent Assembly by the Governor-General, Ghulam Mohammad. The centre subsequently made a concession on the language issue by recognising Bengali as a state language but only in return for the acceptance by the Eastern wing of a centralised state with parity between East and West Pakistan.[63]

The centrepiece of both Mirza's and Ayub's constitution was One Unit, which led to the formation of West Pakistan, a device depicted as purely administrative, to establish Punjabi-Mohajir domination. Ayub Khan talked about the magnanimity that Punjabis must show in accepting only 40 per cent representation in the West Pakistan legislature and not a percentage based on their population.[64] However, the document authored by Mumtaz Daultana, a leading Punjabi politician, in support of the unification of West Pakistan, shows explicitly that it was a vehicle for domination and that it was presented in a manner not to arouse the opposition of the minority provinces. He wrote: 'Punjab must be quiet. At a later stage Punjab will have to take the lead. At that time I hope an effective intelligent Punjabi leadership will have been put in place both at the centre and at Lahore'.[65] The importance of One Unit and parity between the two wings was that it neutralised the Bengali majority in the lower chamber and effectively excluded the Bengalis from power at the centre.

The central government's inflexible response to the Bengali language movement was based on the realisation that recognition of Bengali would result in a loss of opportunities in education and government employment for the Urdu salariat. Ultimately, it would have led to an increase in the Bengali salariat's representation in the bureaucracy and military and the dilution of Punjabi-Mohajir authority within the ruling oligarchy. This would certainly have restricted their attempts to construct a centralised state and their ambitions to expand it by entering into an alliance with the United States. However, the Punjabi-Mohajir alliance was too well entrenched in the incipient state to be deflected from imposing its agenda. The Mohajirs, with 3.5 per cent of the population, had 21 per cent of the jobs in the Pakistan Civil Service and this reflected the group's historic advantages.[66] The Punjabis and Mohajirs were the most vocal advocates of a strong centralised state and were prepared to go to almost any lengths to achieve this goal, including encouraging the army and bureaucracy to destabilise the political leadership.

The exclusion of Bengalis from the centre, the tightening grip of Karachi, the country's political and commercial capital, over East Pakistan, the insensitive handling of the language issue and a growing sense of economic exploitation pushed the eastern wing along the road of separatism. Parity and the language compromise effectively excluded Bengalis from state power. Bengali politicians, mainly from the lower middle class, were unable to exert political power to benefit their constituencies. Parity between the two wings of the country meant that they could not force any measure through the legislature that would benefit East Pakistan. This became even more difficult under the military regime of Ayub Khan, when a system of 'basic democracy' was set up and political parties were not permitted to participate in elections.

The confrontation between the two wings intensified when the Bengali political leadership, led by Mujibur Rahman, was arrested for anti-state activities and charged with treason in the Agartala conspiracy case. The language compromise also effectively excluded Bengalis from national employment opportunities in their own province, as Urdu-speaking Biharis, who had migrated at Partition, populated the positions of petty functionaries in East Pakistan. The language policy permitted Urdu speakers to occupy positions in the East Pakistan Railway or in the Jute industry, which was owned by West Pakistani industrial groups, to the detriment of Bengali speakers. This also had political implications because the civil service heavily regulated the system of basic democracy and those groups that were poorly represented in the bureaucracy found that they did not benefit from the process.[67]

fragmentation of the pakistan salariat

As a consequence of these constitutional shenanigans of the military-bureaucratic oligarchy, the Pakistan salariat, brought together with great difficulty by Jinnah, fragmented into its Urdu and non-Urdu-speaking components. The Punjab had, for historical reasons, adopted Urdu as the language of the salariat instead of Punjabi. In Punjab under Ranjit Singh, like elsewhere in India, Persian was the language of state business. At that time, religious schools taught Gurmukhi and Punjabi was written in a Persian script but its teaching was not widespread. Urdu was adopted as the language of the Punjabi Muslim middle class not at the behest of the Ashraf elite, who were not influential, but of the British. A number of factors influenced their decision. They considered Punjabi to be an uncouth and rustic *patois* of Urdu. They found Urdu convenient, as it was the vernacular used in Hindustan, and in the early period they were keen to discourage Punjabi teaching among the Sikhs. Neither Sikhs nor Muslims showed keenness for Punjabi, as they saw it as providing less employment opportunity than Urdu. The fact that the North-West Frontier Province and British Baluchistan were ruled from Lahore until the early twentieth century resulted in the extension of Urdu in official matters to these areas. After 1887, the British relented in their resistance to Punjabi but support for it was interpreted through the prism of Hindu-Muslim-Sikh rivalry and treated as anti-Muslim.[68]

This historical legacy continued to exercise a strong influence on the Punjabi salariat in Pakistan. Perceptively, Hanif Ramay, a former chief minister of Punjab, points out that the Punjabis exchanged their ethnic identification for a larger Pakistani identification and moved seamlessly between the two, raising fears among minorities of a greater Punjab.[69] This is a common characteristic of many majorities in multi-national states – that they have no ethnicity, which is reserved for minorities. What makes the Punjab unusual is that in order to appropriate Pakistan for themselves they have to articulate their nationalism in Urdu and not Punjabi. The Punjabis were happy to exchange Punjabi for Urdu as it consolidated their domination over Pakistan. By choosing Urdu, however, they cemented the perspective that Punjabi was culturally inferior or non-existent and accelerated the demise of their native tongue. Today, Urdu is the medium of instruction in the Punjab and Punjabi is only taught at the post-graduate level. However, it is alive and well in the bazaar and villages, thus reinforcing the stereotype that it is the language of rustic folk and the *dhaga* (or ox).[70]

In the 1950s and 1960s, there were attempts by visionary intellectuals to revive the use of Punjabi, written in the Persian script, but the elite was not receptive to this development. Their energies were focused on excluding Bengalis from state power and they considered the revival of Punjabi to be a diversionary exercise with potentially serious consequences for their material interest. Promoting the Punjabi language would threaten Punjabi-Mohajir hegemony and undermine their dominance of Pakistan and their control of East Pakistan. This material interest meant that the Punjabi salariat remained wedded to Urdu and uncompromising in resisting the claims of the petty bourgeois Bengali-speaking salariat. This disdain for Punjabi and preference for Urdu also became the basis for the alliance with Mohajirs. However, in spite of the emotional attachment to Urdu, the elite was educated in English. Educational institutions such as Aitchison College or the military academies were English medium institutions, as were colleges of tertiary education in science and technology. Entrance exams to the civil service of Pakistan and the armed forces were also in English. There were several commissions investigating how to increase the use of Urdu, particularly in science and engineering colleges, as well as its expansion within the upper echelons of the establishment. A combination of resistance and inertia, however, meant no reforms were ever introduced to vernacularise state and society.[71] Today, the significance of English in career opportunities is demonstrated by the proliferation of English medium schools, colleges and universities in the private sector. Urdu medium establishments, with the exception of *madrassahs,* have been shunned because they do not equip their students with the fundamental skills required for well-paying professions.

Bengali discontent turned into despondency and rebellion in the face of an uncompromising military-bureaucratic oligarchy convinced of its moral superiority. Class and linguistic differences were reinforced by a racialised discourse drawn from martial race theories propagated during the colonial era. The first crack in the fabric of the state came with the Bengali language movement in the early 1950s in response to Jinnah's decision to make Urdu the national language. The obdurate position taken not only by Jinnah and the leadership of the Muslim League but also by the Nawab of Dacca came as a shock that triggered a major mobilisation in defence of the Bengali language. Attempts to introduce Bengali in an Arabic script and to disparage it for its non-Islamic heritage only further incensed the province. The ill will this produced resulted in a rout of the Muslim League in the provincial elections of 1954.

The victory of the United Front, a coalition of various organisations, including defectors from the Muslim League led by Fazlul Huq, clearly signalled to the leadership of Pakistani nationalism the antipathy its language policy had caused. However, before negotiations could begin, Karachi dismissed the newly elected provincial government on spurious grounds in order to destabilise the opposition. A compromise was eventually agreed, making Bengali a state language on a par with Urdu in exchange for the acceptance of One Unit, and this had a healing effect, but the goodwill was lost when martial law was declared in 1958. Supporters of the central government were projected to do poorly in the pending elections. Suhrawardy was expected to sweep the polls in East Pakistan, with Qayyum Khan winning in the West.[72] The elections, however, were never held and Ayub's subsequent suppression of Bengali culture, including the ordering of Pakistan Radio not to celebrate Tagore's anniversary, only added to their rage.

The suppression of Bengali culture and language strengthened the perception among the Bengali salariat that East Pakistan was being treated as an internal colony. After independence, Pakistan's narrow elite resisted substantive socio-economic reforms and human resource development and opted for an import substitution strategy, as in many decolonised countries. This import substitution strategy, which introduced various regulatory practices to protect infant industries, had several implications. It transferred wealth from the agricultural sector to industry, from the poor to the rich and from East Pakistan to West Pakistan. The strategy resulted in impressive economic growth: there was 6.77 per cent[73] growth in GDP during the Ayub period, which led to the rapid formation of a capitalist class as well as the growth of an industrial working class. This capitalist class, consisting predominantly of Gujarati-speaking Khojas and Memons in Karachi and Punjabi Chiniotis, concentrated enormous amounts of capital in its own hands, including 66 per cent of industrial assets, 70 per cent of insurance and 80 per cent of banking. An oligarchy of some 25-30 families, it accumulated wealth and power completely out of proportion to its small numbers and Bengalis, Sindhis and Baluch were not at all represented.[74]

The Pakistan bureaucracy guided this form of capital accumulation and government regulation of the economy was pervasive. Trading activity was restricted and controlled; exchange rates were overvalued, distorting local markets; financial capital was rationed and the stock market was dominated by the oligarchy. Government intervention in the private sector and in the markets was extensive and as a result of state initiatives, the agricultural sector was transformed from a pre-capitalist to a capitalist economy.[75] The Korean War boom facilitated the strategy. US aid and assistance, both civil and military, also played a central role, following Pakistan's entry into various US sponsored alliances such as the Central Treaty Organisation (CENTO) and the South-East Asia Treaty Organisation (SEATO). However, development remained uneven. It was primarily concentrated in the West, and particularly in Karachi, at the expense of East Pakistan, despite the fact that the eastern wing generated the greatest share of foreign currency through jute exports.[76]

The dash for growth neglected social inequalities and the rising social tension resulted in political instability and ultimately in the break-up of the country. The trickle-down thesis of wealth distribution linked to the 'social utility of greed' proved to be the downfall of the regime. The cost of rapid economic growth was borne by the majority, with rising prices for industrial commodities paid by the rural population. Absolute poverty increased from 8.65 to 9.33 million between 1963 and 1968.[77] East Pakistanis were particularly incensed, as the foreign currency provided by the export of jute, 'the golden fibre', was being re-invested, as a deliberate state strategy, in the industrialisation of West Pakistan, in particular Karachi. This caused huge resentment. Valuable and limited resources were used to fuel industrialisation that did not benefit either the elites or the masses of East Pakistan. Disenchantment with the regime increased in the aftermath of the 1965 war, when foreign investment dried up and agriculture was hit by drought. The Awami League's six points became iconic of the discontent and the party legitimated its demands by reference to the Lahore Resolution of 1940. It countered the strategy of the military-oligarchic elite by demanding regional autonomy and a two-economy model to allow Bengalis greater control over their own resources.

Managing difference has been a major concern for most

nation-states and various strategies have been employed for this purpose, including power sharing and recognising cultural difference. In the case of Pakistan, however, though formally a federation, there has been a history of the centre intervening and suppressing provincial autonomy. The centre's policies have mainly benefited Punjabis and Mohajirs and some Pukhtuns. The Bengalis, Sindhis and Baluch have been largely coerced into silence. Under Ayub Khan's autocratic rule, politicians were banned from political activity through the use of coercive regulations or tarred with the brush of treason, as in the case of Mujibur Rahman and the Agartala conspiracy case. In Sindh and Baluchistan, coercion resulted in ethnic parties such as Jiye Sindh and Ustaman Gall (later merged into the National Awami Party) gaining influence. The resistance went underground during Ayub Khan's military rule and resurfaced with a vengeance in the general upsurge for democracy a decade later.

Ayub Khan's successor, General Yayha Khan, held the country's first free general elections in 1970 but his dilemma was that the elections produced a majority for the Awami League, who if allowed into power would have restructured the state in its own interests. The essential demands of the Awami League for decentralisation, greater representation in the army and respect for a majority decision in the assembly, if accepted, would have undercut the foundation of the Punjabi dominated military-bureaucratic oligarchy. The class difference between the landed and military elites of West Pakistan and the lower middle class Bengali salariat had brought the country to an unbridgeable political chasm.

Faced with this direct, democratic challenge, the ruling elite fell back on coercive tactics. General Yahya ordered a bloody crackdown in the eastern wing, which resulted in an estimated 300,000-500,000 deaths and between two and eight million refugees, mainly into India. The fact that 1200 miles of Indian territory separated East and West Pakistan made this exercise of brute force a futile affair. The acts of genocide and forced migration inflicted upon the Bengali people were justified and rationalised in the name of Islam. The ultimate result, however, was the emergence of Bangladesh, with India's support, as an independent state, with its official ideology based on the Bengali language and culture.[78]

This period witnesses the collapse of the Pakistani salariat into two components, with the different language groups protecting their class interests under the guise of culture. The centre, which was dominated by the Punjabi-Mohajir alliance, replaced the minority rights discourse with a parity discourse to protect its vested interests. The Bengali salariat wanted the recognition of the Bengali language by the state to promote its access to government employment and was enraged that its lack of political control allowed for the economic exploitation of East Pakistan by the West.

West Pakistan was also plagued with anger and discontent against the ruling group. Most of the anger was targeted against One Unit, into which the smaller provinces had been corralled through a combination of coercion and deception. In Sindh, anti-One Unit sentiment combined with opposition to a number of other policies that adversely affected them. The separation of Karachi from Sindh province, the demotion of Sindhi as the state language and the settlement of retired military personnel on land irrigated by the Ghulam Mohammad Barrage, all generated fury against the centre. The fact that Sindhis had low representation in the civil service or the industrial elite meant that they had little influence in the operation of basic democracy and that economic expansion passed them by.

Baluchistan was similarly excluded and Baluch resentment was compounded by the manner of their incorporation into the independent state of Pakistan. Prior to Independence, Jinnah had been the constitutional advisor to the Khan of Kalat and his advice was that the state should demand independence and not join the Indian Union. When Prince Abdul Karim took his advice and declared independence in 1948, the Pakistan authorities enforced its accession to the republic. Abdul Karim opposed martial law in 1958 and in the 1960s the central government was engaged in hostilities with the Zehri and skirmishes with the Bugti tribes. Baluch antagonism against the centre was reinforced by the exploitation of natural resources, such as Sui natural gas, that failed to benefit the local population. Ayub did attempt to mollify Baluch anger by setting up the Quetta Baluch Academy and shifting the cultural locus from Karachi but resentment continued. The Frontier was by comparison more incorporated into the centre, as the Pukhtuns had some representation in the military and bureaucracy and the industrial oligarchy. Pukhtunistan, a claim raised by the Kabul government over the province, had little mileage even among those promoting Pukhtun ethnicity. However, these social and political tensions, exacerbated by the working of One Unit, set the stage for the fall of Ayub and the crisis that led to the emergence of East Pakistan as an independent state.[79]

india as the 'other'

With these internal instabilities, India was constructed as an external 'Other', in opposition to which Pakistan's divided polity could unite. Several writers[80] have convincingly argued that this 'Otherisation' process is a major component of Pakistani nationalism. However, contrary to the view of Ganguly,[81] anti-Indian-ness is not just a post-1971 phenomenon.

After 1947, the bitterness of the Partition legacy and the Kashmir dispute transformed political and religious rivalries into inter-state tensions. Pakistani nationalism portrayed India as its mirror image and inimical to the very concept of a Muslim homeland. This 'good-bad' dichotomy was articulated in terms of history, international relations, religion and culture.[82] At the core of these Indo-Pakistan tensions was the Kashmir issue, which was seen as a continuation of the antagonism between the Muslim League and the Congress over the two-nation theory.[83] It would, however, be a mistake to assume that the Kashmir issue was a uniform influence. Kashmir was only relevant in domestic politics where nationalism was strong – the bastion being Punjab. Where ethnicity was a powerful influence, as in East Pakistan, Sindh and Baluchistan, the Kashmir issue was less significant.[84]

For the military-bureaucracy oligarchy, asymmetry in power relations with India led them into strategic alliances with the USA. Pakistan joined various alliances sponsored by the United States and became a frontline state against the Soviet Union. The same asymmetry was also used to justify military intervention in politics and the suspension of democratic rule. Opponents of the ruling group were constructed as an internal 'Other'. Political forces that opposed centralisation or made demands for internal autonomy for East Bengal were depicted as Indian collaborators determined to undermine the Pakistan state. During the Ayub period, Bengali opposition was painted as un-Islamic and conspiracy proceedings against Mujibur Rahman were designed to undermine his popularity by tarring him with the slur of treason. These methods were used to justify dealing with the opposition as a security issue rather than as political in nature and to avoid the need to negotiate.

pakistan after 1971: islamic versus ethnic nationalism

This section examines two strands in the evolution of Pakistani nationalism after 1971. The first was the changing nature of the centre, which after independence had been dominated by a Punjabi-Mohajir alliance. This alliance, which lay at the heart of the military-bureaucratic oligarchy for more than thirty years, transforms itself in this period. Mohajirs were the original champions of Muslim nationalism but they now found that they were excluded from power at the centre and this led them to construct an alternative imagined community around ethnicity. Simultaneously, Muslim nationalism completes its metamorphosis from a minority rights to a majoritarian discourse. The mantra of one religion, one language and one state becomes the norm.

Prior to independence and partition, Muslim nationalism legitimated itself by opposing what it perceived to be majoritarian impulses within Indian nationalism. After Independence, this discourse was rewritten as a demand for parity to balance East Pakistani electoral dominance in the political process. Post-1971, however, parity was no longer necessary for the Punjabi dominated military-bureaucratic oligarchy and it no longer required the support of the Mohajirs to project its interests. From the 1980s onwards, the Punjabi salariat tenaciously asserted its dominance in the Federation, demanding that the interests of the majority should be a primary consideration for state policy. This somersault led to further re-alignment, fragmentation and conflict among the different ethnic groups in the country.

With the civil war, the break-up of Pakistan, and the emergence of Bangladesh as an independent state, a new round of erasure of the past took place. First, the memories of a united Pakistan were subjected to selective amnesia. The strategic and political blunders that led to the civil war were never publicly discussed. The Hamoodur Rehman Report,[85] which carefully investigated and examined the events and interviewed key personnel involved in the crisis, was suppressed and did not receive a public airing until two decades later. The military-bureaucratic oligarchy closed ranks and refused to accept any responsibility for the political and human crisis that led to the break-up of the country. India became the sole culprit for the debacle and its intervention was held responsible for the emergence of an independent Bangladesh and the humiliating surrender of 90,000 troops. The imposition of a unitary state, the failure to accommodate the Bengali language and culture and the naked economic exploitation of the province were not subject to reflective and critical assessment.

Superficially, Pakistan emerged as a federation of four provinces. One Unit was disbanded, but the new state remained a highly centralised political configuration, which had very limited space for the linguistic and cultural aspirations of ethnic minorities. Biharis, many of whom had joined the para-military forces in support of the army crackdown against Bangladeshi separatism, became pariahs in both countries and were left to languish in refugee camps. One of the few apologies for the tragedy of Bangladesh came from a Pakistani women's group led by Nighat Khan.[86]

The secular credentials of the founder of Pakistan, Muhammad Ali Jinnah, were the second fatality in the process of erasure. In the quest to establish a new Islamic identity, an intensely secular personality was transformed into an Islamic icon whose sole purpose for establishing Pakistan was apparently to create a religious state. Pakistan's military ruler, General Zia ul Huq, attempted to erase from official memory what had become an inconvenient statement made to the constituent assembly by the country's founding father:

'We are stating this fundamental principle that we are all citizens and equal citizens of one State. ... Now I think we should keep that in front of us as our ideal and you will find that in course of time Hindus would cease to be Hindus and Muslims would cease to be Muslims, not in the religious sense, because that is the personal faith of each individual, but in the political sense as citizens of the state.'[87]

This was now considered to be an aberration in the broader context of an Islamic movement for a homeland for Muslims. The secular nature of the Muslim League and the relatively marginal role of the *ulama* in the construction of Muslim nationalism were consigned to the dustbin of history in the best Stalinist fashion.

imagining islamic nationalism

Islamic nationalism imagined a modern centralised theocratic state, armed with all the paraphernalia of war, including nuclear weapons, and had pan-Islamic ambitions. There were two elements to the process. The first was an explicit and very public attempt to Islamise the state and make it superficially compatible with Islamic notions of statecraft. The second, which was equally profound but took place implicitly, was the increasing grip of the military over civil society and the increasing dominance of the Punjabi salariat within state structures. Islamisation and Punjabisation were the dual processes that became so significant with the advent of Zia's military *junta*.

Elements of Islamisation could be found earlier in Zulfikhar Bhutto's premiership. It was a transitional period and his regime expressed continuity with the past as well as making innovations that were adopted selectively by future governments. His innovative use of Islam, making it explicit and connecting it to socialism, was a strategy that was taken straight out of the Muslim League's manifesto of the 1940s. Bhutto's socialist rhetoric articulated social justice within an Islamic framework to address the gross inequalities and multiple forms of deprivation that afflicted the masses on a daily basis. The explicit use of Islam, however, was taken to new heights by the military regime of General Zia ul Huq. He introduced a process of Islamisation, which re-imagined Pakistan as a religious state, with the primary motive to provide the military regime with a fig leaf of legitimacy.

Islamisation justified military rule by attempting to make the Pakistani state compatible with Islamic political theory. It empowered the *ulama* and attracted other groups such as *bazaaris* into supporting the regime. Their influence in Pakistan had earlier been marginal because they had opposed the Pakistan movement and had failed to win significant electoral support. During Ayub's tenure, the *ulama* were divided. In the presidential election of 1965, revivalist elements had supported Fatimah Jinnah's candidacy, while traditionalists, such as the Brelvis and the *pirs,* had supported the military regime. The *ulama* were equally uninfluential during Bhutto's administration, despite their criticisms of his socialistic rhetoric as irreligious. It was only with the Pakistan National Alliance (PNA) Movement, which eventually triggered Bhutto's dismissal, that they began to gain political influence, and this was increased by General Zia's Islamisation policies and the Afghan war. Islamisation was also important for Zia ul Huq's regime in order to finesse the issue of Pukhtun ethnicity, which had the potential to cause political difficulties. The danger was that the arrival in Pakistan of three million, mainly Pukhtun, Afghan refugees would revive the demand for Pukhtunistan. In order to pre-empt this ethnic demand, the military regime promoted the influence of Islamic groups among the refugees and extended Pakistan's influence among the Pukhtun tribes within Afghanistan.

Islamisation under Zia consisted of the introduction of new laws and administrative measures according to conservative interpretations of the Quran and *Sunnah.* It specifically implemented conservative Sunni interpretations of Islam and critics have argued that it led to the 'Sunnification' of the country.[88] It was done in piecemeal fashion and resulted in the Islamisation, to some extent, of the legal system, taxation, finance, media and education, as well as the sciences. The most important innovation was the establishment of the *Shariat* bench of the

Federal Court, which was endowed with the power to strike down any law or administrative ordinance as un-Islamic. For the first time, *ulama* were added to the Federal Shariat Court. However, there were important exclusions to its power, notably the Constitution and Muslim family law. The main emphasis of Islamisation was on punishment and not justice. The Hudood Ordinance introduced Islamic punishments, including amputation, stoning to death and whipping, for a range of offences, including the consumption of alcohol, adultery and theft. The ordinance unfairly focused on women and turned cases of rape into examples of adultery, which were subject to harsh punishments and became the focus of considerable controversy.[89]

An Islamic welfare system was also set up and distributed the proceeds of new Islamic taxes on wealth and agricultural income, *Zakat* and *Ushr*. Collection and distribution of these taxes to the needy required a considerable expansion of bureaucracy. The provincial and national *Zakat* funds required 250,000 people to administer them, and were mostly manned by graduates from the *madrassahs* and seminaries. In a typical year, the National Zakat Foundation spent 55 million rupees, while at the provincial level, 50 per cent of funds were distributed by local *Zakat* committees. 25 per cent were used for scholarships, 10 per cent for supporting *madrassah* students and the remaining 15 per cent went to hospitals and social institutions.[90]

Madrassahs were located in mosque complexes and mainly educated boys between six and sixteen from under-privileged backgrounds. The students memorised Persian and Arabic texts, were taught to read in Urdu, and were given explanations in the vernacular. They were provided with free education and in some cases paid a supplement and granted free accommodation. The popularity of the *madrassah* among the lower middle class increased when *madrassah* certificates were made equivalent to school certificates and *sanads* or final certificates of the Deobandi,

Brelvi, Shiah and Ahl-e-Hadith schools were made equivalent to an MA in Arabic and Islamic studies. This raised the employment prospects of their graduates because for the first time it put Islamic education on a par with secular education. There is considerable debate about numbers of *madrassahs* but it is clear that in the 1980s there was an explosion of them. An estimate from the International Crisis Group puts the number of *madrassah* students at 1.9 million, or over 35 per cent of the Pakistan student population.[91] A recent World Bank report[92] makes a far more conservative estimate, saying that approximately 200,000 children were enrolled full-time in *madrassahs* before 2001, with numbers rising after this period.

The *madrassahs* were no longer producing *ulama* but were churning out the bureaucracy for the Islamic state and cannon fodder for the Afghan *jihad.* The free education on offer attracted students from the lower middle class, from small market towns and deprived and marginalised sectors of society. The reality was that they produced extremely poorly educated men who had received an antiquated education of little relevance to the wider labour market. However, their employment expectations were raised due to state patronage and the role that General Zia's regime gave to these people in the Afghan War. Zia envisaged that they would man the bureaucracy of the Islamic state but the jobs on offer were never sufficient to absorb the majority of the graduates and were cut back with changes in the regime. They were mainly concentrated in parts of the Punjab, the North-West Frontier Province and in pockets throughout the country, such as in Karachi.[93]

Many Islamic activists were given a sense of purpose, importance, respect and authority due to their martial capabilities and involvement in the Afghan war. The Afghan Resistance was based in Peshawar, where each of the main Mujahideen groups controlled refugee camps and had fighters on the ground in Afghanistan. After the Soviet invasion, refugee numbers increased steadily and by 1984 had reached around three million. Over 350 refugee camps were set up in Pakistan, mainly located in the NWFP and Baluchistan. Refugees could only get access to assistance by registering with one of the seven recognised Afghan groups. To qualify for rations they had to settle in a government designated camp. The overall running of the camps was in the hands of the Pakistan civil service, assisted by Afghan tribal chiefs and tribal councils. The Pakistani religious party, Jamaat-i-Islami, had good access to the camps because it was favoured by the authorities. Other Islamic groups were also encouraged to set up schools and *madrassahs*. Islam was emphasised because of the regime's concern to pre-empt the revival of the Pukhtunistan issue. The assertion of Islamic solidarity eventually justified Pakistan's support for the Taliban as a means of exerting Islamabad's influence over the Pukhtun tribes in Afghanistan.[94]

Zia ul Huq's regime attempted to Islamise the Pakistan army officer corps by recruiting student cadres of Jamaat-i-Islami and by the introduction of Islamic teaching and training at the Pakistan Military Academy and at the Command and Staff Colleges. It also took a number of other initiatives to inculcate Islamic perspectives and values in the officer corps.[95] Zia remained, however, very pragmatic and his primary concern was not to divide the armed forces. Consequently, he was extremely tolerant of officers who expressed secular attitudes and behaviour. Such people were not stigmatised or disadvantaged by Zia and hence remained loyal, even when he was trying to inculcate his version of Islamic values in their ranks.

the punjabisation of the salariat

A parallel process of Punjabisation accompanied, out of the

limelight, the more public policy of Islamisation. General Zia ul Huq had very little respect for the different traditions of Pakistan's provinces and no understanding at all of demands for greater provincial autonomy. He stated publicly: 'We want to build a strong country, a unified country. Why should we talk in these small-minded terms? We should talk in terms of one Pakistan, one united Islamic Pakistan.' Ideally, he would have preferred to erase the provinces from the political map of Pakistan and replace them with fifty odd districts, as Ayub Khan had attempted with the basic democracy system. However, he accepted that Ayub Khan's ideas could not be resurrected and that the 1973 Constitution, or at least the principles of federation, had to be adhered to in the interests of national unity. At the same time, he introduced a number of amendments to the constitution to strengthen his own position and that of the army. He also rejected any attempt to limit intervention by the central administration in the affairs of elected provincial governments.[96]

The over-developed characteristics of the Pakistani state[97] and the dominance of the military resulted in the increased influence of the Punjabi salariat. The Punjabisation of Pakistan became much more vigorous under General Zia's rule due to the predominance of Punjabis, particularly in the senior officer corps in the army. Later on, under Nawaz Sharif's premiership, it became even more exaggerated due to the political significance of the Punjab province. For the first time in Pakistan's history, nearly all the most powerful positions were occupied by Punjabis and nearly all the cabinet ministers originated from central and northern Punjab. This was reflected in the diversion of resources to fund major development projects in the province, to the considerable resentment of minority provinces.

General Musharraf, a Mohajir, subsequently removed some of the excesses of Punjabi domination but he did not touch the central features, as they emanated from his power base in the army. Punjabisation is not simply about the numerical domination of Punjabis in Pakistan. It is a reflection of the over-concentration of the Punjabi salariat in the centralised state apparatus, and particularly its predominance in the armed forces. For this reason, suggestions that the division of Punjab into three provinces would rectify Punjabi domination of the Pakistani state are fatally flawed.[98] The Punjabi stranglehold over the military-bureaucratic oligarchy would remain unaffected by the redrawing of political boundaries. Furthermore, redrawing boundaries would open a Pandora's box, as it would increase pressure to re-configure other provinces, particularly the difficult case of Sindh.

The significance of Punjab's multiple relationship with the army is crucial to understanding the Punjabisation process. For historical reasons, going back to British colonial policy, the Pakistan army's recruiting policy still remains narrow and 75 per cent of the army comes from three districts of the Punjab and two districts of the NWFP: Rawalpindi, Jhelum and Attock, Mardan and Kohat. In the Punjab, only the lesser Ashraf elite survived the Sikh wars and the rule of Ranjit Singh, and their close ties to the masses, through their *biraderi* affiliations, made them influential powerful power brokers in the rural areas. They were less wealthy than their counterparts in the United Provinces, but by declaring allegiance to the British Raj in the Indian rebellion of 1857 they were rewarded by incorporation into the colonial structure as semi-official functionaries: *zaildars, lambardars* and honorary magistrates – and by military recruitment. Among Muslims, this recruitment was concentrated in the Jhelum and Rawalpindi districts – what can be broadly characterised as the Potohari region. This was *barani* land, hence poor and sparsely populated, and the principal recruiting ground of the army.

The martial castes of greater Punjab were always closely associated with the state and were able to maintain close relations with successive empires, Mughal, Sikh and British. Under the

British, however, the interlude between the Second Afghan War and the First World War saw a dramatic increase in recruitment from the Punjab, with the majority of soldiers coming from a narrow range of martial castes, representing less than 1 per cent of the subcontinent's population. As a result, the local economy was revolutionised by the multiplier effect of military expenditure. In addition to the direct impact of pay and pensions, the demand for commercial agriculture and domestic handicrafts expanded. Previously inaccessible areas were incorporated into the world economy by the construction of strategic roads, railways, cantonments and by industrialisation. Legislation was also passed to defend the interest of the martial castes. In particular, the Punjab Land Alienation Act of 1900 restricted the expropriation of agricultural land by predatory moneylenders.[99]

Today, the Pakistan army remains the country's biggest employer, with about 550,000 soldiers on active duty and another 500,000 in reserve.[100] It also continues to act as a development agency. The agricultural economy receives continuous stimulation from the demands of the cantonments and the Military Farms Department. The army also generates a relatively sophisticated pool of labour. It trains a large number of drivers, mechanics and engineers, who apply their skill in the civilian economy when discharged. The road transport sector has a significant presence of those who learned their skills in the armed forces.[101]

The Pakistan army has set up a military-industrial complex, which is extremely influential in the Punjab and Pakistan. The Fauji Foundation, the Army Welfare Trust, the Baharia and Shaheen foundations together constitute the country's largest industrial and trading complex. The Fauji Foundation, the largest and oldest of these organisations, has an estimated annual turnover of $500 million dollars, with profits of $40 million dollars. The Foundation owns some twenty industrial and commercial interests and has a major presence in education and health. It runs over a hundred schools and technical and vocational training centres, 12 hospitals and nearly a 100 dispensaries. The Army Welfare Trust manages the Askari Commercial Bank, insurance companies, cement plants and other interests. The Shaheen Foundation runs an air cargo service and TV station, as well as real estate and industrial concerns. These military foundations provide 'womb-to-tomb' benefits for the ex-military men, who run these companies, and their dependents.[102]

Officer loyalty has been carefully nursed by all military regimes but the influence of the military in civilian life has increased substantially in recent years. Under General Ayub Khan's rule the military handed the administration back to the Civil Service within a relative short period of time. Ayub Khan was careful not to offend the bureaucracy, as it was responsible for the day-to-day running of the country. This arrangement was radically changed during General Zia's regime, when he asserted the authority of the military over the civil administration by nominating military personnel to the top positions in the federal and provincial bureaucracies and state-owned institutions.

This process has been more vigorously pursued by General Musharraf's regime in order to maintain the loyalty of the armed forces. In a low key but persistent manner, it has effectively reduced the civil service to a subordinate position in the running of the country. The Prime Minister's Secretariat, Civil Service Training Institution, the Federal Service Public Commission, the Ministry of the Interior, the Establishment Division, Federal Public Service Commission, the National Accountability Bureau, Ministry of Information Technology, all have serving or retired generals in key positions. Official state organisations such as the Pakistan Olympic Association, Athletic Association of Pakistan, Pakistan Cricket Board, Pakistan Hockey Federation and some Universities have also had senior military officers running them.[103]

It is simplistic to argue that military rule is synonymous with Punjabi domination and that all of Punjab is a beneficiary of this process. Within the Punjabi speaking regions of Pakistan, many social and linguistic groups do not have a significant presence in the military bureaucratic oligarchy, most notably the Siraiki-speaking peoples of South West Punjab. The Siraiki-speaking areas, principally around Multan and Bahawalpur, have made a conscious and explicit attempt to distance themselves from dominant groups in the Punjab. The British classified Siraiki as a dialect of Sindhi and Riyasati, Multani, Lahnda and other Western dialects as Punjabi. This classification persisted in Pakistan and was repeated in the 1951 and 1961 censuses. In 1981, however, during Zia's regime, Siraiki was reclassified as a separate language. The consequence was that for the first time Punjabi was not the majority language in the country. 9.8 per cent of the total population reported that they spoke Siraiki and 14.9 per cent of the Punjab's households declared their self-identification with Siraiki. This made them the fourth largest linguistic group in Pakistan.[104]

The first conscious effort to revive the language in which Khwaja Ghulam Farid rendered his mystical hymns was in the 1930s. But as a result of Partition, migratory waves of refugees from East Punjab arrived in Multan, swelling the population and eventually dominating the city's industrial and commercial sectors. Their presence undermined the efforts of the Siraiki speakers to establish the city as a cultural centre for Siraiki. For the refugees Lahore was their cultural centre. A continuing sense of deprivation, however, contributed to the development of the Siraiki movement in the 1960s. A variety of literary organisations and journals emerged at that time but the movement remained cultural in character. It was unable to take advantage of the political space provided by the downfall of Yahya Khan and made no demand for a Siraiki-speaking province. Its cultural agenda varied from persuading Radio Multan to increase transmission time in Siraiki to the activities organised by the Siraiki Academy.[105] But there has recently been a shift back to politics, with two organisations becoming active – the Pakistan Siraiki Party and the Siraiki Qaumi Movement.[106]

The other area of dissent within the Potohar region is Azad Kashmir, that part of the former princely state which is administered by Pakistan. Pakistan describes the area as administratively autonomous but in practice most decisions are cleared by Islamabad. Unlike other parts of the Potohar region, Mirpur was not, generally, a recruiting area for the British Indian Army. Instead, Mirpuris established a niche in the engine rooms of the British merchant navy, which in the post-war era allowed them to establish a bridgehead for chain-migration to Britain. Substantial numbers of Mirpuris left their ships and called their families and clansmen to join them in a great wave of migration. It is estimated that well over 50 per cent of the 687,592 Pakistanis settled in Britain, are from Mirpur and neighbouring Kotli.[107] In many villages, over half of the population is resident abroad, resulting in significant flows of remittances back to their families. Paradoxically, however, while this has produced a short-term increase in the standard of living in Mirpur, it has not led to sustained economic growth. The Mirpuris deeply resent the fact that their considerable financial contribution is not being deployed to stimulate the economic and infrastructural development of Mirpur or Azad Kashmir. Neither has the Mangla Dam, which was built in the 1960s, generated proportionate benefits for the local population. While electricity was being supplied down stream as far as Karachi, the neighbouring villages were only connected much later. This frustration boiled over in the short lived Dadiali Rebellion, which was put down by

Pakistani paratroopers but served as a reminder of the discontent among Azad Kashmiris.[108]

The boundaries between Mirpuris and Potoharis are largely artificial in cultural terms and there are few, if any, linguistic or cultural differences between those living on either side of the river Jhelum. However, Mirpuris assert that they are Kashmiri and hence not Pakistani or Punjabi. This sense of Kashmiri identification has been fed by a growing number of grievances against the government in Islamabad mixed up with sentiment that makes rule from Muzaffarabad equally undesirable. In some quarters, this has resulted in a desire for real freedom, as expressed in the slogan 'Kashmir Zindabad! Pakistan Murdabad!'[109] Thus when insurgency took off in the valley of Kashmir in 1989, it found strong support from the Jammu Kashmir Liberation Front (JKLF), which was founded amongst Mirpuris in Birmingham. Mirpuris in the UK also led the demand for linguistic recognition for their language. It was in the UK that the first attempts were made to develop written examples of the language and that lobbying of the BBC's Asian Network resulted in programmes in Mirpuri for the community.

imagining a new mohajir identity

The Punjabi salariat for historical reasons associated the Urdu language with sophistication and career opportunities, and in the early days of Pakistan there was a cosy relationship between the Punjabi and Mohajir elements within the ruling oligarchy. This was disrupted in the 1980s, largely as a result of the Soviet intervention in Afghanistan, by the incorporation of Pukhtuns into the military-bureaucratic elite. As a minority, with a history of political opposition to the Pakistan demand, the Pukhtuns had been excluded from power for more than twenty years after Partition. In the 1970s, Prime Minister Zulfikhar Bhutto had used coercion to deal with the National Awami Party and the Jamiat-ul-Ulama-i-Islam, which had formed a coalition in the North-West Frontier Province after the 1970 elections. At that time, Bhutto had incarcerated the Awami party leader, Wali Khan, on trumped-up treason charges and had succeeded in alienating the Pukhtuns. He had also provoked a major rebellion in Baluchistan by dismissing its elected government, which resulted in nearly 9000 deaths and the deployment of 80,000 troops.[110]

When the Russians marched into Kabul at the end of 1979, the North-West Frontier Province became far more significant for Islamabad. Under the military government of General Zia, there was a re-alignment of political forces both at the centre and in the centre's relationship with the western provinces. Concern that Pakistani support for the *mujahadin* would provoke Soviet-Afghan attempts to destabilise Baluchistan encouraged General Zia to co-opt or pacify the Baluch tribes and their political leaders. Baluch suspicions were not easily allayed but the centre's efforts did make them neutral to Islamabad in this period. In the North-West Frontier, the establishment found its task much easier, as the arrival of Afghan refugees swung public opinion in the province in favour of Islamabad's strategy against Kabul. As the province was the West's main conduit of weapons, resources and finance for the Afghan guerrillas, the army incorporated more Pukhtun generals into the ruling clique. The fact the Pukhtuns were already relatively prominent in the army made this task much easier and Pukhtun generals and bureaucrats came to play a significant role in the military regime. This inclusion, however, was to some extent at the expense of Mohajirs – both in the army and the civil service. The shift against Mohajirs had been initiated during Bhutto's time – particularly in Sindh – but expanded rapidly during Zia's rule. Punjabi and Pukhtun influence in Karachi both in the administration and in business increased considerably and Mohajir influence in the civil service was limited by the quota system.[111]

This resulted in alienation and the search for alternative political strategies by some elements of the Mohajir community. The Mohajirs had historically been the strongest supporters of Pakistan's nationalism but once alienated they began to – 're-imagine' themselves as an ethnic minority. This shift from nationalism to ethnicity can be explained in terms of the theory of relative deprivation. Relative deprivation is the difference between expectations, or what a collectivity feels it is entitled to, and what it actually receives. Belief in relative deprivation at a collective level, due to either increased expectation or a decline in rewards, can result in an identity-based mobilisation and the potential for violence.[112]

The change in the fortunes of the Mohajirs, from junior partners in the military-bureaucratic alliance to an increasingly excluded element, turned them into challengers to the Establishment, who frequently resorted to violence in the 1980s and 90s. This alienation mainly affected the lower middle-class Mohajirs. The elite Mohajirs, as English-speakers, remained incorporated within the establishment. The lower middle-class Mohajirs, who spoke exclusively in Urdu, were already finding their employment opportunities restricted by the quota system imposed by Zulfikhar Ali Bhutto. Under pressure from the Sindhi language movement, Bhutto had recognised Sindhi as a provincial language and imposed a quota on the entry of Urdu mother tongue speakers into the Pakistan Civil Service. The quota remained in place even when Bhutto was removed from power and during Zia's reign Mohajirs suffered increased competition from Pukhtuns.[113]

Mohajir identification is an example of a new ethnicity, which does not fit into classical anthropological understandings of ethnicity based on culture.[114] Anthropologists have traditionally argued that ethnicity is based on kinship groups and culture in its widest sense, which incorporates religion and language. There are new forms of identity politics, however, that do not fit into these criteria, such as the emergence of black and gender politics. New ethnic identities are contested, contingent and assert themselves intermittently but persistently.[115] These identities are more flexible, more open, less predictable, and less dependent on inherited traditions.[116]

'Mohajir' was a term used originally to describe all those who had migrated from India to Pakistan at the time of Partition. The majority of migrants were from East Punjab and they settled in West Punjab but in the imagining of Mohajir ethnicity these Punjabi Mohajirs are excluded. The term 'Mohajir' is reserved for non-Punjabi migrants who settled in urban Sindh, and includes both Urdu and Gujarati speakers. The Urdu speakers originated from Uttar Pradesh, Bihar and Hyderabad, and are united only by language and by the courtly culture associated with these states. They display variations in dialects and cultural norms; they practise endogamy and rarely marry outside their particular sub-group; and exhibit significant sectarian differences, primarily between Sunni and Shiah. The Gujarati speakers are a smaller group, which includes trading communities settled in Karachi before and after Partition. Gujaratis are not homogeneous. There are numerous subdivisions according to dialect and locality, as well as sectarian differences. All these divisions, however, within the Gujarati and Urdu speaking communities and between Sunni and Shiah, were submerged in the newly imagined Mohajir identity.

Mohajir self-awareness was born on the university campuses in the late 1970s and early 1980s in opposition to other student associations, which were organised on linguistic and regional lines. The All Pakistan Mohajir Students Organisation (APMSO) was formed in 1978 and many of its members, including its leader, Altaf Hussain, were originally members of the the Islami Jamiat-ul-Talaba (IJT), the Student Wing of the Jamaat-i-Islami, who had become disillusioned with it because it was a Punjabi dominated organisation. APMSO played a very active role in the Pakistan National Alliance movement against Bhutto in 1977 but subsequently broke with it because it failed to deliver on its promises to help the Mohajirs regain political and economic control in urban Sindh.

In 1984, the Mohajir Qaumi Mahaz (MQM) was formed to represent the political interests of the community and by August 1986, at its famous Nishtar Park meeting in Karachi, it was attracting hundreds of thousands of supporters. Once its hold over the Mohajirs was established, the MQM operated as their sole representative on the political stage. In 1987, it had a landslide victory in the local bodies elections in Hyderabad. In 1988, it swept the Mohajir constituencies in the general elections, at the expense of the Islamic parties, and became a coalition partner with the Pakistan Peoples Party (PPP) both at the centre and in Sindh. However, the MQM's association with Sindhi groups broke down in October 1989, resulting in bitter and violent ethnic conflict, primarily in the city of Karachi. The coalition with the PPP had been sustained by their common hostility towards the Punjabi and Pukhtun populations of Karachi, but they had few shared interests. Relations deteriorated when the PPP was unable to deliver on a major MQM demand for repatriation of Biharis from Bangladesh for fear of a Sindhi backlash.

The MQM then entered into an alliance with the Islami Jamhoori Ittehad (IJI), the main national opposition to the PPP, led by the Punjabi politician, Nawaz Sharif. It now toned down its anti-Punjabi, anti-Pukhtun rhetoric and because of its opposition to Benazir Bhutto increased its hostility towards Sindhis. The conflict between the MQM and the Sindhis reached such a pitch that in May 1990 it persuaded the Chief of Army Staff, General Aslam Beg, to ask the President to remove the PPP government.

The MQM partnership with the IJI Government from 1990 to 1992 was a period where it flexed its muscles and exercised enormous street power, maintaining an iron grip on public activity in Karachi and Hyderabad. The newspapers were frequent targets of MQM's armed workers, who disrupted publication and distribution on the slightest pretext. In June 1992, exasperated by the violence and chaos that became so common in Karachi and Hyderabad, the Pakistan army launched 'Operation Clean Up' to restore law and order in the province. The leadership of the MQM, including Altaf Hussain and members of the National and Provincial Assembly, went underground and the army encouraged a revolt of the Haqiqi faction against Altaf's leadership. The MQM boycotted the 1993 National Assembly elections in protest against the army operations but participated successfully in the Sindh Assembly elections. The army was withdrawn from Karachi in December 1994 but what followed was a year of attacks by MQM militants on the civil administration in the city. This led in July 1995 to a new operation, launched by the Interior Minister in the PPP Government, General Babar, who used a mailed fist to crush the MQM rebellion.

In the 1997 elections, the MQM again joined hands with Nawaz Sharif and established a coalition government in Sindh for the third time. However, this failed to bring peace to the city, as MQM activists released from jailed were hungry for revenge, which resulted in a new spiral of violence and chaos. By 1998, the coalition had fallen apart over the murder of philanthropist, Hakim Saeed, and the party was once more in the political wilderness. After General Pervez Musharraf's military coup in October 1999, the MQM was again under pressure. However, with the holding of provincial and national elections, the party was rehabilitated and included in the ruling administration with a presence at the local, provincial and national level.[117]

india and the USSR as the 'Other'

In the 1980s, pan-Islamism began to play an important role in Pakistan's international relations. The main axis of this ideology was the construction of India and the USSR as the 'Other'. An anti-Indian ideology continued to forge strong national consensus within the military-bureaucratic oligarchy and among political elites. This resulted in the privileging of security over and above all other issues, including development, education, health, food security and the environment. Consequently, security became the main justification for the pre-eminence of the military, both in terms of resources and of its intervention in the political process.[118]

The anti-Soviet dimension increased when Pakistan became a frontline state against the USSR and acted as a conduit for weapons, training, and resources for the Afghan insurgents. Subsequently, the pan-Islamic ideology of *jihad* developed during the Afghan conflict was deployed in Kashmir, where the same strategy of low intensity conflict used successfully against the USSR became the model, the *modus operandi,* for intervention from the late 1980s onwards. The Islamic groups declared *jihad* against India and juxtaposed Islamic Pakistan against Hindu India. Negative portrayals of India and of Hindus also featured in school texts, where a deliberate falsification of history showed the emergence of Pakistan as the inevitable product of Islamic identity. During the Afghan conflict, the Urdu press in particular nurtured a most vitriolic Islamic rhetoric, which was subsequently turned against India in support of the Kashmir cause. Thus, the rise of an Islamic version of nationalism exaggerated existing racialised stereotypes of India and of Hindus. This *jihadi* nationalist rhetoric was tacitly pro-US until 9/11 and the intervention in Afghanistan, when it became hostile to the United States.

Internally, this same process at various times targeted

Sindhis and Mohajirs, who were portrayed as pro-Indian, and justified their suppression with extreme prejudice. Pan-Islamism was in fact a Sunni phenomenon and in this formulation Shiahs were classified by some *jihadi* organisations as non-Muslims. Shiahs were accused of being agents of Iran, particularly during Zia's regime. They were subject to violent attacks by radical Sunni groups, who would not accept them as part of a wider Islamic community. Ahmaddiyas and Christians were also subject to harassment, threats and attacks. For the MQM, both of these modes of thought were problematic. Accusations that the organisation was pro-Indian were usually the justification for its brutal suppression. The sectarian dynamic also had the potential of disrupting Mohajir cohesion, as both Shiahs and Sunnis were members of this imagined community. Consequently, MQM was one of the few political organisations that openly declared itself to be non-sectarian.[119]

conclusion

In opposition to conventional understanding of national and ethnic movements in Pakistan, which sees them as essentialist and fixed categories, I have argued that identities are imagined and re-imagined through the interaction of three factors: culture, agency and structure. As these variables change over time and place, new identities are constructed and become pertinent because of the changed context. In the first phase of Muslim nationalism, from the late 1930s onwards, it emerged as a minority rights discourse. The Western-educated, English-speaking Muslim elite was able to draw the Urdu-speaking salariat into mainstream Muslim nationalism. This was a secular discourse that attempted to defend Muslim class interests, which were being eroded or threatened by non-Muslims and by Indian nationalism specifically. The main thrust of this movement was to create a coalition out of many disparate groups and to make it an effective opposition to Indian nationalism by portraying it as predatory and communalist. Ideological agreement was far more difficult but the main objective was to reinforce provincial authority against a strong centre. This minority rights discourse runs through all the various currents and strands within Muslim nationalism and the Muslim League's main concern was to promote various forms of constitutional reform that would consolidate the decentralisation of power and not necessarily push for the separatist option. This option was only favoured by a minority and was only accepted by Jinnah once all other alternatives were exhausted.

In the second phase, after Partition and Independence, this fragile coalition quickly unravelled, as the Urdu salariat and the new political elite dropped decentralisation and minority rights and pursued a one-language policy based on a highly centralised state. The Mohajir leaders were dependent on the state for political survival, as they had no natural political constituency in the country they founded. They, therefore, promoted a discourse of parity between the two wings of Pakistan, which prevented the ascendancy of the East Bengal political leadership, both constitutionally and, more importantly, within the military-bureaucratic oligarchy. This resulted in a clash between the Punjabi-Mohajir salariat and the Bengali salariat, which found support from the other ethnic minority salariats of West Pakistan, who continued to campaign for a decentralised polity. The class difference between the centre, which was run by an elite upper middle-class, and the lower middle-class Bengali salariat, made compromise difficult. The inability to accommodate different class and language interests ultimately resulted in the demise of Muslim nationalism, the break-up of Pakistan and the emergence of Bangladesh.

With the demise of a united Pakistan, Muslim nationalism mutated again and Islamic nationalism came to be promoted by the military regime of General Zia. Islamisation was intended to provide some legitimacy for the regime by strengthening support for the intervention in Afghanistan and acting as a counterweight to the demands of the different ethnic salariats within Pakistan. The fact that it drew support from the same lower middle-class constituencies, which were involved in ethnic politics, meant that it provided the regime with a breathing space. However, Zia's public commitment to Islamisation disguised the creeping Punjabification of the state. In this phase, the country's rulers performed an ideological somersault from a minority rights to a majoritarian discourse. Any ideological link with the Muslim nationalism of the pre-Partition period was discarded and inconvenient historical facts, such as the secular nature of Jinnah's political views, were airbrushed from history. The incorporation of the Pukhtuns into the ruling oligarchy also resulted in the alienation of Mohajirs, who responded by forming an ethnic organisation to protect their interests. By the late 1980s, the original prime movers of Pakistani nationalism had jettisoned the official ideology and claimed to be an ethnic minority. While there has been some political re-incorporation of Mohajirs by General Musharraf's regime, this has not addressed the underlying grievances that led to the formation of Mohajir ethnicity.

Throughout Pakistan's sixty-year-old history, Islamabad's approach to diversity has been cynically to co-opt or coerce groups that have not been accommodative. This approach has often resulted in considerable violence and sown deep distrust between the centre and the country's ethnic groups. If Pakistan is to become a more equitable society, alternative strategies need to be considered that incorporate all groups and increase cohesion and affinity with the centre. There is a need to imagine a new discourse that actively incorporates excluded and marginalised groups. Ultimately, this requires a process of political negotiation and has to go hand in hand with the strengthening and deepening of the democratic process.

There is also a pressing need for the refinement and enrichment of the concept and practice of federalism and a move away from the present system, which favours Punjab by distributing resources on the basis of population. Sindh's complaint (stemming from the importance of Karachi as the country's main commercial and industrial centre) has been that tax generation should be given greater recognition. Baluchistan's point, as the country's poorest province, is that levels of poverty should be taken into account. There are some signs of movement on these points by the present regime. However, in a country which devotes so many of its resources to the armed forces, the budget for the social sector remains far too limited to satisfy the growing demands of the burgeoning population. Punjab, the largest province and the main recruiting ground for the army, continues to receive the lion's share of resources to the detriment of other provinces. There have been suggestions that the dominance of Punjab could be diluted by splitting it into three provinces but this will not affect the real source of Punjabi power which stems from the pre-eminence of the Punjabi salariat within the military-bureaucratic oligarchy. This salariat becomes even more powerful when authoritarian rule is the norm and not democracy.

In Pakistan, where democracy is the exception rather than the rule, incorporation into the military-bureaucratic oligarchy has often seemed the main route to power for excluded groups. Democracy has never been well enough established for the working of the ballot box to provide power and resources to those beyond the ruling elite and its allies. Indeed, on occasions when elections have resulted in the empowerment of such groups, whether at provincial or national level, they have rarely been allowed to complete a full term of office. The pursuit of imagined new identities to the point of rupture, secession and violent upheaval – whether in Bengal or elsewhere – has been a function of authoritarian rule, which has proved incapable of delivering a state in which all its citizens have confidence.

Has India done any better? The fault lines of nationhood have run similar courses in both countries. Issues of decentralisation, provincial autonomy, and ethnic identity have featured prominently in India too, and in recent years, India's secular polity has come under siege from forces of Hindu revivalism, which share some of the same social and economic roots as Pakistan's Islamist politicians. What Pakistan has not experienced, however, is empowerment through the ballot box of long suppressed castes and communities, a function of India's well established democracy and of real transfers of resources to new political forces. If Pakistan is a long way from achieving this empowerment, it is in large measure because of its dysfunctional oligarchic system of government and neglect of the social sector, which has been ruthlessly squeezed by the emphasis on national security.

If Pakistan is to achieve a more stable and just polity, and a national consensus on the benefits of citizenship, it must begin with a rational and reasoned debate on national security. Such a debate will need to widen the concept of security to incorporate human security and to consider how resources for social development can simultaneously be increased and access for subaltern groups improved. A functioning and robust democracy and improved relations with India would play an important role in facilitating this process.

NOTES:

1   I.H. Qureshi, *The Struggle for Pakistan*, University of Karachi (Karachi,1969).

2   Joseph Stalin, *Marxism and the National and Colonial Question*,

English edition, A. Fineberg ed. (London,1936)

3   See Harrison for a full discussion of the different Baluch positions. Selig S. Harrison 'Ethnicity and Political Stalemate in Pakistan' in Banuazizi, A. &.Weiner, M. eds, *The State, Religion, and Ethnic Politics: Pakistan Iran and Afghanistan* (Lahore, 1987)

4   A.K. Brohi, 'Apropos of the Wisdom of our Brother Bizenjo', *The Dawn*, 9 October 1978.

5   Craig Calhoun, *Critical Social Theory: Culture, History and the Challenge of Difference* (Oxford, 1995), p. 193.

6   Eric Hobsbawm, and Terence Ranger, *The Invention of Tradition* (Cambridge, 1983).

7   Benedict Anderson, *Imagined Communities* (London, 1983).

8   Craig Calhoun, *Critical Social Theory: Culture, History and the Challenge of Difference* (Oxford, 1995).

9   Stuart Hall, 'Politics of Identity', in T. Ranger, Y. Samad, O. Stuart eds., *Culture, Identity and Politics: Ethnic Minorities in Britain,* (Aldershot, 1996)

10   Benedict Anderson, *Imagined Communities* (London, 1983)

11   Ernest Renan, 'What is a Nation?' in Homi Bhabha ed., *Nation and Narration* (London, 1990)

12   Terence Ranger, 'Introduction' in T. Ranger, Y. Samad, O. Stuart, eds., *Culture, Identity and Politics: Ethnic Minorities in Britain* (Aldershot,1996)

13   Hamza Alavi, 'Politics of Ethnicity in India and Pakistan', in Hamza Alavi & John Harriss, eds, *Sociology of 'Developing Societies': South Asia* (Basingstoke, 1989).

14   Ibid.

15   Craig Calhoun, J. Gerteis, J. Moody, S. Pfaff, & I. Virk, 'Introduction to Part IV', in *Contemporary Sociological Theory,* (Oxford, 2002), p. 189.

16   Tariq Rahman, *Language, Ideology and Power: language-learning among Muslims of Pakistan and North India* (Karachi, 2002), pp. 40-1.

17   Anthony Giddens, *A contemporary critique of historical materialism* (Cambridge, 1985), pp. 119-21.

18 John Stuart Mill, (1861) *Consideration on Representative Government*, cited in Will Kymlicka ed., *The Rights of Minority Cultures* (Oxford., 1996), p. 5.

19 Frederick Engels, (1849) 'Hungary and Panslavism' cited in Will Kymlicka ed., *The Rights of Minority Cultures*, (Oxford, 1996), p. 5.

20 John McGarry, & Brendan O'Leary, *The politics of ethnic conflict regulation: case studies of protracted ethnic conflicts* (London,1993)

21 Gowher Rizvi, 'Ethnic Conflict and Political Accommodation in Plural Societies: Cyprus and Other Cases,' *Journal of Commonwealth and Comparative Politics*, Vol 31, No 1, (March 1993)

22 Ayesha Jalal, *Democracy and authoritarianism in South Asia — A comparative and historical perspective* (Cambridge, 1995)

23 I.H. Qureshi, *The struggle for Pakistan* (Karachi,1969)

24 Asim Roy, *The Islamic Syncretistic Tradition in Bengal* (Princeton, 1983), pp. 19-20, 33; Peter Hardy, *The Muslims of British India* (Cambridge, 1972), pp. 8-10.

25 Peter Hardy, *The Muslims of British India* (Cambridge, 1972), pp. 17-18.

26 D.J. Matthews, C. Shackle & H. Husain, *Urdu Literature* (London, 1985), pp.4-11.

27 Peter Hardy, *The Muslims of British India* (Cambridge,1972), pp. 18-19.

28 Sumit Sarkar, *Modern India: 1885-1947* (Delhi, 1983); Hardy, Peter, *The Muslims of British India* (Cambridge, 1972).

29 'Addresses Presented in India to His Excellency the Viceroy and the Right Honourable Secretary of State for India,' *Parliamentary Papers*, 1918, vol 18 (Cmd 9178), p. 564. Indian Statutory Commission (1930) Vol. 1 (Cmd 3568), pp. 27-30.

30 Asim Roy, *The Islamic Syncretistic Tradition in Bengal* (Princeton, 1983), pp. 26-8, 58-60.

31 Tariq Rahman, *Language and Politics in Pakistan* (Karachi, 1996), p.49.

32 Hamza Alavi 'On Religion and Secularism in the making of Pakistan', Text of Prof. Karrar Memorial Lecture on 2 November

2002 in Karachi, http://www.sacw.net/2002/HamzaAlavi
Nov02.html

33   National Documentation Centre, Criminal Investigation
      Department (hereafter NDC, CID), S 358, 'The Ahrar Movement
      in Punjab,' pp. 25-6, 58-61. NDC, CID, Sc 359, 'The Ahmadiya
      Sect,' pp. 15-1615-16.

34   'Nehru to Prasad, 21 July 1937, in V. Choudhary ed., *Dr Rajendra
      Prasad Correspondence and Select Documents,* New Delhi, i, p.66.
      Choudhary Khaliquzzaman, *Pathway to Pakistan* (Lahore,1961),
      p.62.

35   Indian Office Records (henceforth IOR)Mss. Eur. F 115/2B (Haig
      Collection), Haig to Linlithgow, 7 May 1937, ibid., Haig to
      Linlithgow, 24 May 1937.

36   Yunas Samad, *A Nation in Turmoil — Nationalism and Ethnicity in
      Pakistan, 1937-1958* (New Delhi, 1995) p.56.

37   IOR, L/P&J/8/686 Coll. 117/E1 (Muslim Grievances under
      Congress Ministries, 1939-42) Haig to Linlithgow, 10 May 1939.

38   Ibid.

39   IOR, L/P&J/8/686 Coll. 117/E1 (Muslim Grievances under
      Congress Ministries, 1939-42) Replies from the Governors of
      Bihar, Central Province and the United Provinces to Governor-
      General's enquiries on Muslim grievances.

40   IOR, Mss. Eur. F 125/104 (Linlithgow Papers). Hallet to
      Linlithgow, 29 September 1941.

41   Ahmad, A. Khan, *The Founder of Pakistan: Through Trial to
      Triumph* (London, 1942), pp. 19-20; IOR, L/P&J/8/690. Coll. 117-
      E-4-B (Pakistan), Craik to Linlithgow, 4 March 1941.

42   K.K. Aziz, *Rahmat Ali: A Biography,* (Lahore, 1987), pp. 199-201.

43   Sikander Hayat, *Outlines of a Scheme of Indian Federation,*
      (Lahore. no date); Sayed Abdul Latif, *The Cultural Future of India,*
      (Bombay, 1938); National Archives of Pakistan, Quaid-i-Azam
      Papers (hereafter NAP, QAP), F/49 Mohammad Afzal Qadri to
      Jinnah 25 June 1939. 'A Punjabi', *A Confederacy of India* (Lahore,
      1939); K.K. Aziz *A History of the Idea of Pakistan* (Lahore, 1987).

44   *India's Problem of Her Future Constitution,* preface by M.A. Jinnah,

(Bombay, 1940).

45   *Muslim League Sessions 1940 and the Lahore Resolution* compiled by Ikram Ali Malik, National Institute of Historical and Cultural Research (Islamabad, 1990), pp. 280-89.

46   Abul Hashim, *In Retrospection* (Dacca, 1974), p.109-110.

47   *Muslim League Sessions 1940 and the Lahore Resolution* compiled by Ikram Ali Malik, National Institute of Historical and Cultural Research (Islamabad, 1990) p.295.

48   Harchandrai Vishindas, Chairman, Reception Committee, Annual Session, Indian National Congress at Karachi, 1913, in H. Khuro, ed., *Documents on the Separation of Sindh from Bombay Presidency, Islamabad,* (1982) i, p.1; G.M. Syed, in *Sind Legislative assembly Debate* (1943), Karachi, 3 March 1943, pp. 18-19.

49   S. A. Rittenberg 'The Independence Movement in India's North-West Frontier Province 1901-1947', (PhD Columbia University, New York, 1977).

50   NAP, QAP, F274/141, Abdullah Haroon, Chairman, Foreign Committee, AIML, to Jinnah 23 December 1940; K.K. Aziz, *A History of the Idea of Pakistan* (Lahore, 1987), p.651.

51   Ian Talbot 'Planning for Pakistan: The Planning Committee of the All-India Muslim League 1943-46', *Modern Asian Studies,* (1994), 28, 4. p.882.

52   NAP, QAP, F/49 Mohammad Afzal Qadri to Jinnah 25 June 1939.

53   NAP, QAP, F204/324-329, Confederacy of East Pakistan and Adibistan, 1944; Abdul Mansur Ahmad, *Fifty years of Politics as I saw it (Bengali)* (Dhaka, 1975) *pp 242-3, 287-9.*

54   Record of Interview between Mountbatten and Liaquat, 10 April 1947, in N. Manserghed. The Transfer of Power 1942-47 (thereafter TP) HMSO, London, X, pp331-32.

55   NAP, QAP, F 565/101, Mazhar Inam, Chairman of the Provisional Migration Committee to Jinnah, 12 November 1946.

56   National Documentation Centre, Criminal Investigation Department (hereafter NDC, CID), S 415(Punjab Police Secret abstract of Intelligence), No. 24, Sutton, 14 June 1947, p.307.

57   Note of meeting between the Cabinet Delegation, Wavell and

Suhrawardy, 8 April 1946, in Record of interview between Mountbatten and Suhrawardy, 26 April 1947, *Transfer of Power documents*, HMSO, London, x, p.448

58   Ayesha Jalal 'Inheriting the Raj: Jinnah and the Governor-General Issue', in *Modern Asian Studies*, 19,1, (1985) pp. 43-9.

59   NAP, QAP, F 10/51-54, 'The Organisation of the Pakistan Government by Liaquat Ali Khan', 6 July 1947.

60   Khalid bin Sayeed, *The Political System of Pakistan*, (Boston, 1967).

61   *Report of the Court of Inquiry Constituted under the Punjab Act II of 1954 to enquire into the Punjab disturbances of 1953* (1954) Lahore, p.203.

62   Public Record Office, Dominion Office Papers (hereafter PRO, DO) 35/5107B, UK High Commission to Commonwealth Relations Office (CRO), & January 1953. PRO. DO. 35/5300, Murray to Swinton (CRO), 12 January 1953.

63   'M.L. Acceptance of Regional Autonomy Reported (Muree [sic] Pact), 10 July 1955,' in H.H. Rahman, ed., *History of the Bangladesh War of Independence* (Dhaka, 1982) i, p. 430.

64   Ayub Khan, *Friends Not Masters: A Political Biography* (Karachi,1967)

65   Mumtaz Daultana (no date) 'One Unit Document', Section B, p.1; Section D, p.6.

66   R. Braibanti, *Asian bureaucratic Traditions Emergent from the British Imperial Tradition* (Durham, 1966), p. 269.

67   Richard Sisson and Leo. E. Rose, *War and Secession: Pakistan, India and the Creation of Bangladesh* (Berkeley,1990); National Archives, United States, Records of the Department of State, Relating to Internal affairs of Pakistan, 195-59, record series 790D.00, Group 59 (hereafter NAUS, RG 59), Box 4144, 790D.00/2-2752, Withers to the Department of State, 18 November 1950.

68   Tariq Rahman, *Language and Politics in Pakistan* (Karachi,1996)

69   Cited in Feroz Ahmed, *Ethnicity and Politics in Pakistan* (Karachi, 1998), p.xix.

70   K.K. Aziz, *A History of the Idea of Pakistan*, (Lahore, 1987), p.206-8.

71 Tariq Rahman, *Language and Politics in Pakistan* (Karachi,1996)

72 Yunas Samad, *A Nation in Turmoil—Nationalism and Ethnicity in Pakistan, 1937-1958,* (New Delhi, 1995) chapters 4 & 5.

73 *Pakistan Economic Survey, 1996-97,* Government of Pakistan (Islamabad,1997)

74 A. M. Weiss, *Culture, Class, and Development in Pakistan — The Emergence of an Industrial Bourgeoisie in Punjab* (Lahore, 1991), p.34.

75 S. Akbar Zaidi, *Issues in Pakistan's Economy* (Karachi, 2000), second impression.

76 Ibid.

77 Ian Talbot (1998) *Pakistan: A Modern History* (London, 1998), p.171.

78 Richard Sisson and Leo. E. Rose, *War and Secession: Pakistan, India and the Creation of Bangladesh* (Berkeley, 1990), pp. 306, 297.

79 Ian Talbot, *Pakistan: A Modern History* (London,1998)

80 Jean-Luc Racine, 'Pakistan and the 'India Syndrome': Between Kashmir and the Nuclear Predicament' in Christophe Jaffrelot ed., *Pakistan — Nationalism without a Nation?* (Delhi, London, 2002); Mohammad Waseem 'The Dialectic between Domestic Politics and Foreign Policy' in. Christophe Jaffrelot ed., *Pakistan — Nationalism without a Nation,?* (Delhi, London, 2002)

81 Sumit Ganguly, 'The Islamic Dimension of the Kashmir Insurgency' in Christophe Jaffrelot ed., *Pakistan — Nationalism without a Nation?* (Delhi, London, 2002)

82 J. Korbel, *Danger in Kashmir* (Princeton, 1954), p25.

83 G.W. Choudhury, *Pakistan's Relations with India 1947-1966* (London,1968)

84 W.J. Brands 'Pakistan's Foreign Policy: Shifting Opportunities and Constraints,' in Ziring, Braibanti and Wriggins eds., *Pakistan: The Long View* (Durham N.C.,1977), p.401

85 *The Report of the Hamoodur Rehman Commission of Inquiry into the 1971 War — As Declassified by the Government of Pakistan* (Vanguard Books., Lahore, no date)

86 Interview with Dr Nighat Khan, Executive Director ASR, 28

December 2004.

87 'Inaugural Speech of Quaid-i-Azam in the Constituent Assembly',in G.W. Choudhury ed., *Documents and Speeches on the Constitution of Pakistan* (Dacca,1967), p.21.

88 S.V.R. Nasr, 'Islam, the State and the Rise of Sectarian Militancy in Pakistan' in *Pakistan — Nationalism without a Nation?* edited by Christophe Jaffrelot (Delhi, London, 2002)

89 Hasan Askeri-Rizvi, 'Pakistan in 1999 – Back to Square One' in *Asian Survey.* Vol. XL, No.1, January/February 2000, pp.208-218; Ayesha Jalal,,'The Convenience of Subservience: Pakistan', in Deniz Kandiyoti ed., *Women, Islam and the State* (Basingstoke,1991)

90 Jamal Malik, *Colonialization of Islam — Dissolution of Traditional Institutions in Pakistan* (New Delhi, 1996), p.144.

91 ICG Pakistan: Madrassahs, Extremism and the Military, ICG Asia Report (Islamabad/Brussels,2002)

92 Andrabi T., Das, J., Khwaja, A.J., Zajonc, T., *Religious school Enrolment in Pakistan: a Look at The Data*, World Bank, WP 3521, Washington D.C. (July 2005)

93 Ibid.

94 Weinbaum, M. G., *Pakistan and Afghanistan — Resistance and Reconstruction* (Oxford, 1994), pp. 54-9.

95 A. Hussain, *Strategic Issues in Pakistan's Economic Policy* (Lahore, 1988), pp 361-364.

96 General Zia-ul-Huq cited in Selig S. Harrison, 'Ethnicity and Political Stalemate in Pakistan' in Banuazizi, A. &.Weiner, M. eds., *The State, Religion, and Ethnic Politics: Pakistan Iran and Afghanistan* (Lahore, 1987),p.254

97 Hamza Alavi 'Authoritarianism and Legitimation of State Power in Pakistan', in S. Mitra, ed., *The Post-Colonial State in Asia* (London, 1990); Ayesha Jalal, *The State of Martial Law* (Cambridge. 1985)

98 Ian Talbot, 'The Punjabization of Pakistan: Myth or Reality?' in Christophe Jaffrelot ed., *Pakistan — Nationalism without a Nation?* (Delhi, London, 2002); Ahmad Faruqui ,'Inter-provincial rivalries and national security' *Daily Times*, Site Edition, Wednesday, 1 December 2004.

99   Clive Dewey ,'The Rural Roots of Pakistani Militarism' in D.A. Low, ed., *The Political Inheritance of Pakistan* (Basingstoke, 1991), pp. 271-4.

100 www.pakistanidefence.com/PakArmy/CommandStructure.htm

101 Clive Dewey, 'The Rural Roots of Pakistani Militarism', in D.A. Low ed., *The Political Inheritance of Pakistan* (Basingstoke,1991).

102 *The Dawn* 2nd December 2001.

103 The News International, 6 April 2006, www.jang.com.pk' /thenews/apr2006-daily/06042006/metro/i16htm; Zahid Hussain, 'A Military State', Newsline, October 2004

104 Feroz Ahmed, *Ethnicity and Politics in Pakistan* (Karachi, 1998), p.234-5.

105 C. Shackle, 'Siraiki: A Language Movement in Pakistan', in *Modern Asian Studies*, 11 March 1977.

106 R. Bakhsh,' The MQM's New Clothes', *The Herald*, January 1994.

107 Census, April 2001, Office for National Statistics (ONS) http://www.statistics.gov.uk; Census, April 2001, General Register Office for Scotland (GROS) http://www.gro-scotland.gov.uk .

108 Roger Ballard, 'The Kashmir Crisis: A view from Mirpur,' in *Economic and Political Weekly*, March 2-9, 1991.

109 Ibid.

110 Selig S. Harrison, 'Ethnicity and Political Stalemate in Pakistan' in Banuazizi, A. &.Weiner, M.eds, *The State, Religion, and Ethnic Politics: Pakistan Iran and Afghanistan* (Lahore,1987)

111 Yunas Samad, 'Reflections on Partition: Pakistan Perspective' in Ian Talbot and Gurharpal Singh eds, *Region and Partition: Bengal, Punjab and the Partition of the Subcontinent* (Karachi,1999).

112 Gurr, T. R., *Why Men Rebel* (New Jersey,1974)

113 Yunas Samad, 'Reflections on Partition: Pakistan Perspective' in Ian Talbot and Gurharpal Singh eds., *Region and Partition: Bengal, Punjab and the Partition of the Subcontinent* (Karachi,1999)

114 Stuart Hall, 'Politics of Identity', in T. Ranger, Y. Samad, O. Stuart, eds, *Culture, Identity and Politics: Ethnic Minorities in Britain* (Aldershot,1996)

115 Sue Benson, 'Asians have Culture, west Indians have Problems:

discourses of Race and Ethnicity in and out of Anthropology' in T. Ranger, Y. Samad, O. Stuart eds., *Culture, Identity and Politics: Ethnic Minorities in Britain* (Aldershot,1996)

116   Stuart Hall, 'Politics of Identity', in T. Ranger, Y. Samad, O. Stuart eds, *Culture, Identity and Politics: Ethnic Minorities in Britain* (Aldershot,1996)

117   Yunas Samad, 'Reflections on Partition: Pakistan Perspective' in Ian Talbot and Gurharpal Singh, eds., *Region and Partition: Bengal, Punjab and the Partition of the Subcontinent* (Karachi,1999); Iftikhar Malik, 'Ethno-Nationalism in Pakistan: A Commentary on Muhajir Qaumi Mahaz (MQM) in Sindh', *South Asia*, XVIII, no 2. (1995)

118   Yunas Samad, 'Military and Democracy in Pakistan', in *Contemporary South Asia3* (3), (1994) pp 189-201

119   Idrees Bakhtiar, 'United They Stand'? Herald, July 1997.